katrin
cargill's

curtain
bible

simple & stylish designs for
contemporary curtains & blinds

special photography by david hiscock

quadrille

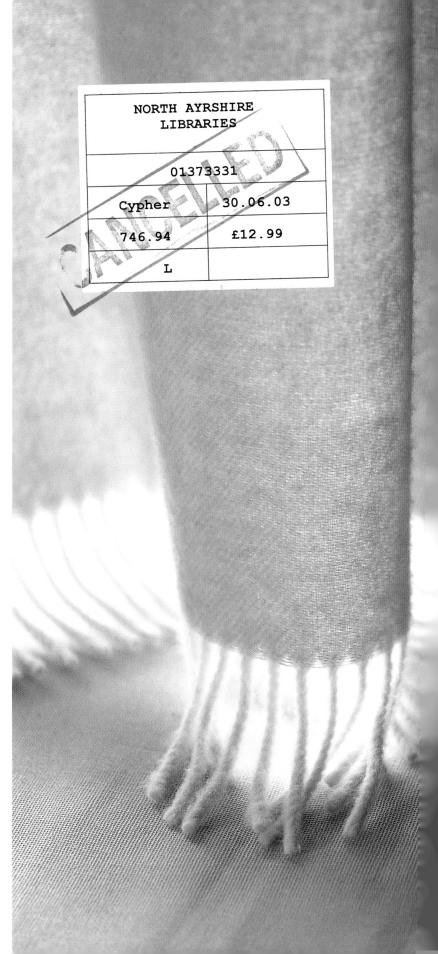

For David and Harry,
my big rock and my little rock

First published in 2001 by
Quadrille Publishing Limited
Alhambra House
27–31 Charing Cross Road
London WC2H 0LS

This paperback edition first published in 2003

Text and projects © Katrin Cargill, 2001
Design and layout © Quadrille Publishing Ltd, 2001
Special photography © David Hiscock, 2001
Illustrations by Lizzie Sanders

Creative Director Mary Evans
Editorial Director Jane O'Shea
Art Director Françoise Dietrich
Project Editors Nicki Marshall and Alison Moss
Picture research Nadine Bazaar
Production Nancy Roberts

British Library Cataloguing in Publication Data
A catalogue record for this book is available from the British Library

ISBN 1 84400 021 4
Printed and bound in Singapore

part I

questions

This section of the book explores the different types of windows, looks at their inherent features and potential problems, and offers solutions for dressing them. It leads you through the initial decision-making process, looking at how you can create different effects with curtains, correct architectural anomalies, control issues of light and privacy, and use colour, pattern and texture successfully.

Consider your windows. Look at them; study their appearance in relation to the room. Do they occupy a large proportion of wall space or are they small rectangles punched into the wall? Are they part of the architecture of the room such as a bay window or a dormer window? Start by learning to identify the different types of windows, as this will narrow down your options for the type of curtains you choose.

Sash windows open vertically by means of sash cords, and are surrounded by an architrave or moulding. Casement windows can be double or single, and usually open outward. Both types lend themselves to a variety of treatments. French windows and doors, however, often open into the room, which presents a problem for curtains and blinds. Curtain poles and tracks need to be set wide and high enough over the French window to allow the fabric to stack away when the window is opened. Blinds can work, but either need to pull high and clear of the window, or be specially made to fit each individual frame. Bay windows consist of a series of windows that extend out from a wall either in a curve or a rectangle. If the windows are sash or outward-opening casements, you can install a track or pole with brackets to fit so that the curtains neatly follow the bay. Where such windows open into the room, each one will need its own blind or curtains that stand clear of the openings.

The key to walls of glass, sliding doors and large loft windows is to obscure as little of the architecture and view as possible. Concealed tracks, pull-up roller blinds, and external shutters or blinds all work well in these situations because their practical designs allow the architecture to take centre stage. Likewise, circular and arched windows are beautiful architectural features in their own right, which are best left unadorned. Dormer windows can be dressed with curtains on portière rods which pivot and can lie flat against the side walls when open. They can also be dressed with individual roll-up blinds. Dormer windows which are slanted are best treated with a curtain on tracks fitted top and bottom.

Whatever the challenge of curtaining a window presents, try and solve it in the most logical and simple manner – the more complicated the solution, the more likely it will be the wrong one.

types of window

above

Casement windows display an impressive range of curtain designs.

right

The exterior of a window can reveal much about our style inside.

overleaf

The variety of shapes and sizes of windows is vast and curtains are not always called for.

creating the effect

Once, long ago, we knew exactly what to do with a window. Householders in the eighteenth century essentially left their windows bare. Material was too expensive to be used in any lavish way, so Georgians (except for the vastly rich) were content with a frill above the window, or cotton strung across the middle, and relied upon shutters for privacy and warmth. As fabric became more readily available and cheaper in the nineteenth century, window dressing became de rigeur with lace portières, rouched blinds, bales of patterned silk and cheerful printed cotton creating layer upon layer of drapery and adding to the assortment of patterns and textures in a room. For many of us, that's still the solution – covering a window in layers and tassels and swags like a well-iced cake, with the first layer almost inevitably 'nets'. One of the reasons for this stems from a very practical need: old houses have old windows – and old windows are often draughty.

In the twenty-first century there is a new way of looking at curtains and what they can bring to a room. This development is partly prompted by technology – there are better ways to keep ourselves warm than draping heavy fabrics against every window. Double glazing and central heating allow us to lighten up and uncloak our lives. And with this freedom comes a shift in focus to the effect we would like to create. Do we want high drama or simple serenity? Do we prefer a classic treatment or something a little more idiosyncratic to put a personal stamp on the room?

These days anything goes. Fashion trends and the availability of a vast range of materials allow us to choose fabrics and patterns, new accessories and trimmings for window treatments that might startle our grandmothers but perfectly suit today's easier lifestyle, with its quest for the exotic as well as the familiar. And the same freedom of choice applies to hardware. Tension wire kits with eyelets are virtually supermarket items and can modernise a room instantly. Multi-track gliding panel systems mean versatile control of windows from a translucent covering during the day to total blackout. Double track systems render elaborate pelmets almost superfluous. The knock-on effect is that we need much less fabric, which allows us to buy the exquisite taffeta we couldn't afford before, or go to the other extreme and make 'throwaway' curtains that we can change with the seasons.

right

The drama of a tricolour banner curtain makes a stunning statement in a room with a glorious high ceiling. It complements the eclectic pieces of modern furniture.

overleaf left

Vintage dresses hung at the window allow the owner to display her collection and achieve a unique window treatment that creates privacy.

overleaf right

The understated patterns in sheer fabrics work well in contemporary interiors that favour clean lines and natural materials.

Look around at what inspires you, what influences your taste, and head out to the local department stores to research the wealth of fabrics, trimmings and curtainalia on offer.

With the right combination of style and fabric, we can immediately establish a room's atmosphere and mood. We can select curtains that draw the focus to the window by using strong colours and patterns next to more neutral furnishings. We can set the style by complementing period furniture with a sympathetic curtain design. We can make the windows recede into the background if they are unattractive or offer an uninspiring view, with softer colours and an understated design. Now, more than ever, we can combine function with beautiful textiles.

left Vibrant floor-length curtains create a fantastic impact in a warehouse apartment and serve both as room dividers and window coverings.

overleaf left
A sheer balloon shade projects glamour with a period chandelier.
overleaf right
A canvas panel with a few judiciously placed appliqués of homespun cotton give the appearance of a painting.

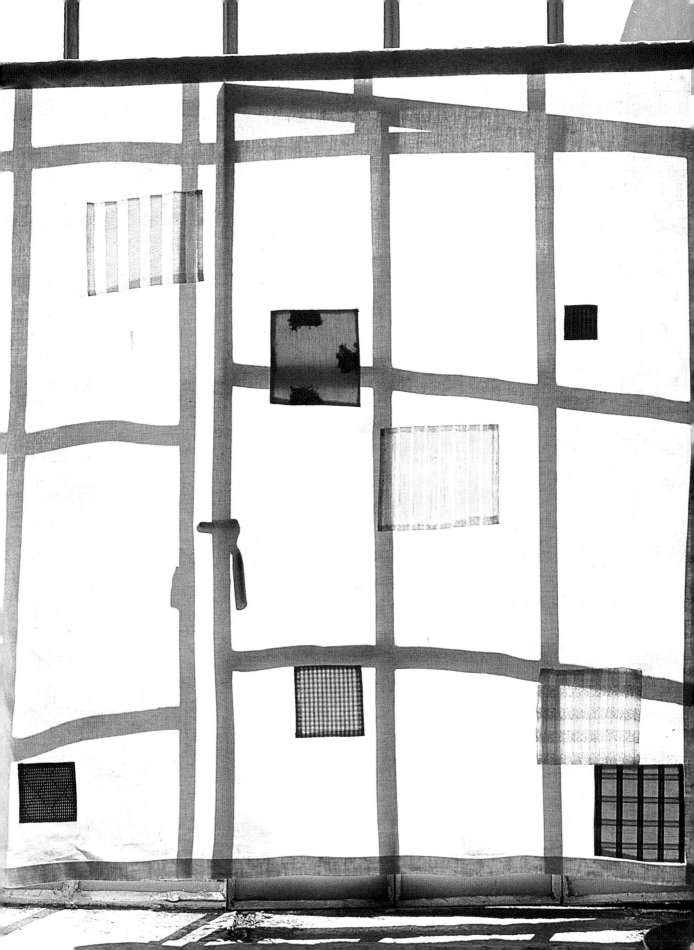

practicalities

Besides their importance in the overall look of a room, curtains are valuable tools in creating a space that's easy to live in. With the right length or width of treatment, you have the opportunity to correct awkward proportions, unify a design scheme, and temper or invite in the light. The problem-solving ability of curtain-making is vast, and a few tricks of the trade will let you make the most of the windows you've got. The first step is always to live a while with your windows, watching where the light falls, thinking about how you use the room, and what architectural concerns you'd like to cure.

correcting proportions

Sometimes a room feels all wrong; the colour may be beautiful, details unique, the furniture just the thing but the room itself continues to bother you. It might feel unbalanced, asymmetrical or simply uncomfortable in an elemental way. Once, architects built from plans that recreated the symmetries of classical architecture – the Georgian certainty created rooms of proportion, based on an almost mathematical rule. But these days, we might well live in an old house which has undergone years of unsympathetic tampering, or in a new house with uninspired architecture, and could be faced with windows that are not in harmony with the room. There is no real rule of thumb, your eye will tell you that something is not right: perhaps the windows are too narrow for a wide wall or too large for a small room.

previous pages left
A double-height window is emphasized with vast floor-length curtains edged in a strong black and white horizontal stripe.

previous pages right
Laid-back cotton muslin panels, individually hung on French windows, tumble to the ground and complement the muslin-wrapped chairs.

right
Floor-length curtains are deliberately hung high over the window to give a greater sense of height to the room.

from the left
A low casement window gains visual height by the high placement of a swag.

Another trick for adding height – a pelmet board is hung close to the ceiling.

Differently sized arched-top windows are unified by the careful placement of straight wooden poles and the use of plain fabric.

Choosing an appropriate window treatment allows you to shift the attention within the room and settle the atmosphere. A common problem encountered is windows that are set too low on a wall. If you were to put curtains just over the top of the actual window this would emphasize the problem. Raising the top of the window treatment well above the window will create the illusion that the window is taller. Make certain, if you are putting up a valance, that the bottom edge is lower than the top of the window, or you will create a worse problem than you began with! If you have a window that looks too narrow for the room, extend the pole or tracks a little on either side so that your treatment is wider than the window. A window that looks too wide for a room is best left with a blind or a curtain of a very lightweight material with little fullness. A series of windows with different heights is best unified by curtains of the same drop.

physical challenges

Occasionally, especially where a room has been insensitively remodelled, a window will jut almost into a corner, leaving little or no room for a pole or track, let alone a finial. The solution is to use a blind that will draw the eye away from the problem or use a pole with disc finials (see the project on p122). Solutions I do not advocate are using a pole with a finial on one end and extending the pole straight into the wall on the other side, or a 'half' pelmet that butts into the wall – all these do is draw the eye to the problem!

An attic with dormer windows can present a unique problem. In this case, portière rods come into their own. These swinging rods open right back against the wall. Alternatively, blinds can work well:

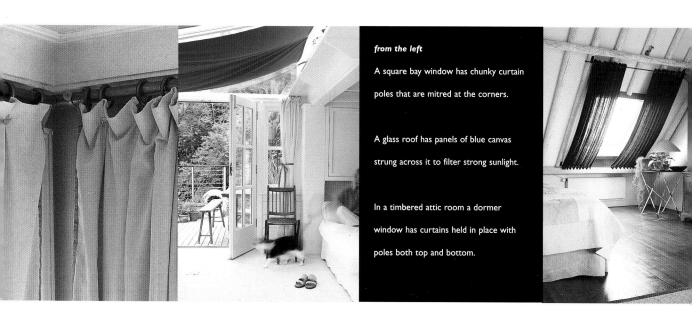

from the left

A square bay window has chunky curtain poles that are mitred at the corners.

A glass roof has panels of blue canvas strung across it to filter strong sunlight.

In a timbered attic room a dormer window has curtains held in place with poles both top and bottom.

if the window opens inwards, attach the blind to the window frame so that it will swing open with the window without obstruction. Bay windows can be treated in many ways, but often curtains block a lot of light at the sides, just because of the volume of fabric in the stack back. You might consider extending the pole or track out of the bay and onto the walls, or use a lightweight fabric that will take less space, in conjunction with blinds, or use blinds only and no curtains. Arched and circular windows present yet another challenge. On the whole, circular windows are small architectural statements set high on a wall and need no covering. For arched top windows, curtains with conventional headings can be made to follow the curve and fixed to a curved lath, but the headings would have to be caught together permanently and either held back with brackets or Italian stringing at the point where the curve stops. Straight poles with curtains or shutters that are set across the top of the semi-circle also work well.

filtering the light

Though the prime purpose of a window is to admit light and air and, with luck, a pretty view, sometimes there can be too much of a good thing. Work towards a window design that admits plenty of light; sunlight is such a buoyant presence in our lives. But controlling light is important too, to preserve fine furnishings, for instance, or to prevent glare on a computer screen or work area in a home office. This is where layers are not an unnecessary frivolity. By combining an inner curtain of a translucent material with shutters or heavier curtains that draw, you can diffuse the light entering the room. Look, too, at cultures that live with more sun than we do for ideas of materials to use: louvred shutters from the south of America or France, for instance, where any degree of darkness from

from the left

Inward opening casement windows in the eves of a house are treated individually with little Roman blinds.

To hide the unattractive top and side of this window, a fringed wool blanket is folded over and sewn with a pocket to take an expansion pole.

shadow to stygian can be achieved with a fingertip. Cane blinds, bamboo or matchstick blinds, or venetian blinds all afford a choice of shade, as well as heat protection.

These same tools will help when you crave total darkness as an option. Perhaps you need to protect a sleeper, or do work that requires a blackout. The traditional heavy lined and interlined curtains certainly will do the trick, but looking to more minimal treatments there are good alternatives. Blackout lining, which used to be thick, rubbery, and stifling, has evolved; it is now both lightweight and easy to sew, and thus allows air to circulate. In many hot climates tight-fitting external wooden shutters are closed to the sun all day and only thrown open early in the morning or evening: no other window covering is needed. Other traditional solutions include Holland blinds which are cleverly used in Scandinavian countries during their bright nights of summer. These roller blinds are made from tightly woven cotton that has been treated with oil or shellac. Again, layers at the window will allow you to pick the depth of darkness you want to achieve. Conversely, layers will also help when it is warmth that you are seeking against draught coming through older windows, or to muffle sound if you live on a busy road. Interlining is available in many weights and thicknesses to enable you to resolve these issues.

right A beach bungalow has billowing curtains at the double doors that diffuse strong sunlight, yet allow the breeze to circulate, and protect from prying eyes.

from the left

A crisp and tailored semi-opaque blind complements this minimal style bathroom and creates privacy without cutting out the light.

Slatted white wooden blinds allow a remarkable amount of light to pass into the room.

privacy

Privacy is a personal issue; some of us live more easily with our lives on display, while for others, being able to shut out the world is the very essence of home, especially at night. It is important to survey your home from the outside as night falls, to get an idea of where the architecture acts as a veil, or the plantings provide some cover, or whether everything is illuminated. Net curtains have fallen into disuse, and perhaps that's a good thing, as they often become grey and lifeless after a few washings. There are some

above A simple bunk room in a hot climate has blackout Roman blinds to block out the light in the early hours of the morning.

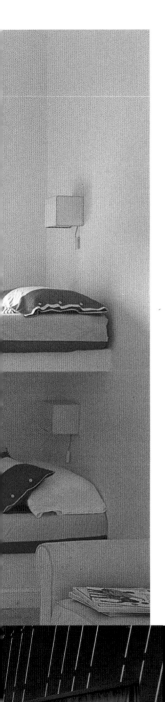

innovations that make sense, such as the blind that sits at the bottom of the window and is designed to be pulled half way or all the way up. Café curtains work equally well running across the middle of the window. Other solutions mean getting to work on the window itself. Opaque glass will give you a permanent solution that will temper the light and block the gaze of those outside, as will etched glass, to be found now designed with polka dots or stars, to give a more decorative look to the window.

dual-purpose and screens

Solutions for window treatments can also be brought into a room to help define a space that is meant to serve more than one purpose: a home office that also has to act as a dining room or a bedroom, for example. One-room living is not uncommon, and raises its own problems of privacy, light and organization that curtains and screens can be drafted in to solve.

Running a curtain across a room lets you carve up space in a whole new way. Consider a loft, a great expanse of space with, often, endless rows of windows; in this case internal curtains or screens can act to provide privacy and light control, as well as shape the space for adaptable living. Blackout curtains can carve out a thoroughly private space, while double tracks and tension wires allow you to hang a curtain almost anywhere. Does a cupboard have to be made of wood, or would a tent of fabric or a curtained recess be enough? Curtains that pull can be used to screen a child's welter of possessions, then open up for play (and provide the place for all those impromptu plays, as well).

from the left

A heavy canvas curtain doubles as a door, allowing air to circulate.

A pull-up roller blind is useful for maintaining privacy while letting in light and a view.

Heavy floor-length curtains can be drawn to prevent draughts from under large doors.

choosing fabrics

Having chosen your style of curtain, it is important to consider the intrinsic qualities of fabrics, as each type will give a different finished look. Probably the most common cloth is a woven cotton. It comes in plains, can be printed on, or has a pattern woven into it. Cotton is hardwearing, inexpensive, drapes quite well, and is practical in terms of laundering. However, if you are looking for a soft flowing, billowing fabric, cotton is not the answer. Look instead at taffeta, silk or man-made equivalents. Cotton also shrinks, so

from the left

French doors are fitted with two types of treatment for different requirements.

A pivoting screen protects from strong sun and wind.

Consider an alternative to a door. Here a hallway is screened off with a curtain.

left A sleeping area is screened off with a curtain made from a contemporary sheer fabric that does not shield the light.

make sure you buy it pre-shrunk, or wash it before you make up the curtain. Silks, satins, taffetas and many man-made fibres possess excellent draping qualities and are available in a huge range of plains and patterns. Natural silks tend to rot or give out under strong sunlight after a time if not properly lined, and thus can be an expensive proposition. Linen and linen union (a mixture of linen and cotton) are the most hardwearing textiles. Generally, the more expensive ones are better finished, drape beautifully, and feel softer.

Trimmings provide a useful final touch. The key is to use them minimally and with care. A narrow picot braid can outline the leading edges of a pair of curtains and give them a crisper feeling. Trimmings are best used to pull in a colour to finish a room. A little goes a long way, yet adds a personal stamp.

colour, pattern, texture, sheers

Pattern, colour and texture are so intertwined that it is hard to talk about one without mentioning the others. When it comes to pattern, unless your personal taste really is for large multi-coloured prints, it is best to stick with a two-colour print. The variety in just two colours alone is huge, and it will be simpler to co-ordinate other fabrics and colours. Patterns work best in isolation: in other words, plain painted walls around printed curtains bring out the best in both; conversely, a patterned wallpaper is best set off with plain curtains. A small pattern isn't necessarily less busy than a big one, it is the way the pattern is used. The best guide when learning to use pattern is to pick one you like, and pull out a colour from it (this can be white) to use liberally. This will isolate the pattern and accentuate it. Pattern also works well with a simple check or stripe as its foil: thus a busy blue and white toile de Jouy blind is best complemented with a check in the same colours for upholstery. Remember also that pattern exists in a weave, such as damask, just as successfully as in a print, and sometimes a weave can be more subtle.

For those who dislike too much pattern and print, texture can provide the interest and variety needed in a room. Modern textiles have the benefit of the latest technology so man-made fibres can produce the most luscious tactile weaves and textures. Velvets, chenilles and double-stitched fabrics feel wonderful and last for years. Many woven textiles are reversible and are great labour savers when it comes to sewing. Imagine machining a lovely pair of curtains in an afternoon that need no lining or interlining, and look great from the outside as well!

Another area of great innovation is in sheers and translucent textiles. These fabrics come in a glorious range of colours and styles from those with pockets to display items, such as pressed flowers, to those woven from metallic thread.

The subject of colour is a vast area of insecurity and intimidation to many. I tend to take a fairly simplistic attitude to this, namely, use only the colours you love. Remember that the important rule is not the colour you use but how you use it, and what sets it off. A room painted navy blue could look oppressive, but add white curtains trimmed in navy, and white upholstery and you have a crisp and sophisticated room. Red is a difficult colour to work with, and I adore red. Again, use it sparingly and put plenty of another colour such as white or cream with it; this will make it pop out but not overpower.

The colour palettes shown on this page are drawn directly from the projects in Part 2 of this book. They illustrate the versatility within a single colour scheme. With the individual colours used in different degrees, the combinations can create a completely new effect in each setting.

For example, the red and white striped scalloped curtains on p136 have the same red as the mitred panel on p54, the difference being the surrounding colour or pattern.

The aqua blue of the double curtains on p58 is the same as the blue in the self-valance curtains on p110. But look how the effect changes when it is put with different colours. Being aware of these possibilities should help you to discover your palette and make it work for you.

neutrals

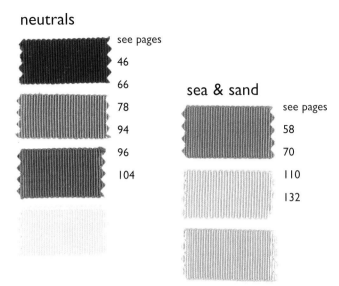

see pages
46
66
78
94
96
104

sea & sand

see pages
58
70
110
132

greens

see pages
122
152
156

tricolor

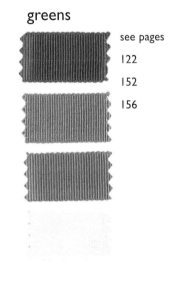

see pages
54
62
74
136
140
144
148
158

lilacs

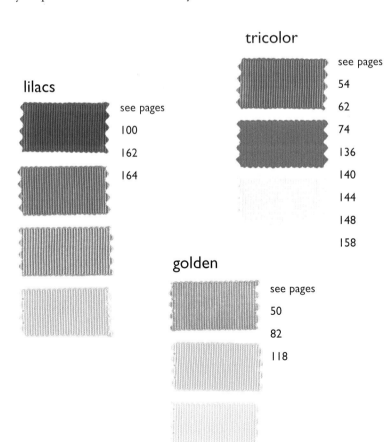

see pages
100
162
164

golden

see pages
50
82
118

following pages

The following pages illustrate how easy it is to use pattern, by focusing on the variety in two-colour prints; texture, in creating interest through weave and trimmings; and the simple elegance of sheer fabrics that need no further decoration.

pattern

texture

sheers

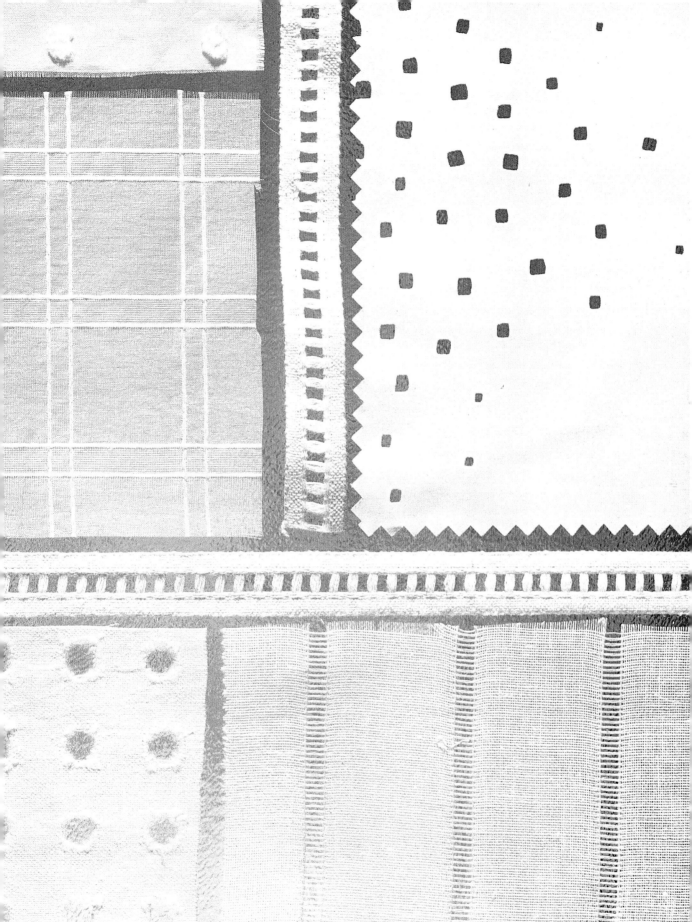

part 2
solutions

Now for the ideas, the inspirations, and the nitty-gritty details! This section includes a range of projects, which span the simplest roller blind that can be made from a kit, to lining and interlining a curtain, together with detailed instructions for making them. There is a comprehensive array of methods and sewing techniques woven throughout. You can use these projects as they are, following the instructions given or interpreting them to suit your own needs and tastes, or show them to your curtain maker to illustrate the type of curtain you are looking for.

Today's interiors achieve their pared-down, streamlined look not just by less clutter but also by innovative technology in hardware. The serene mood that is created by large open spaces filled with light and a few perfectly placed pieces of furniture is the embodiment of modern style. Thanks to a large array of curtainalia on the market, the minimal look is easier to achieve than ever, from tension wire and eyelet kits to versatile double-track systems in anodised chrome. Many of these new systems take the place of traditional pelmets and valances that can give a sense of heaviness to a window. Minimal window treatments require less fabric, as a rule, so you can choose the expensive organdie you might have passed by before. The message in this chapter is to use bold design and simple shapes have a little fun!

contemporary

The window treatments illustrated on these pages embody the

contemporary style. The projects, which begin overleaf, offer various

interpretations of the look for the modern home.

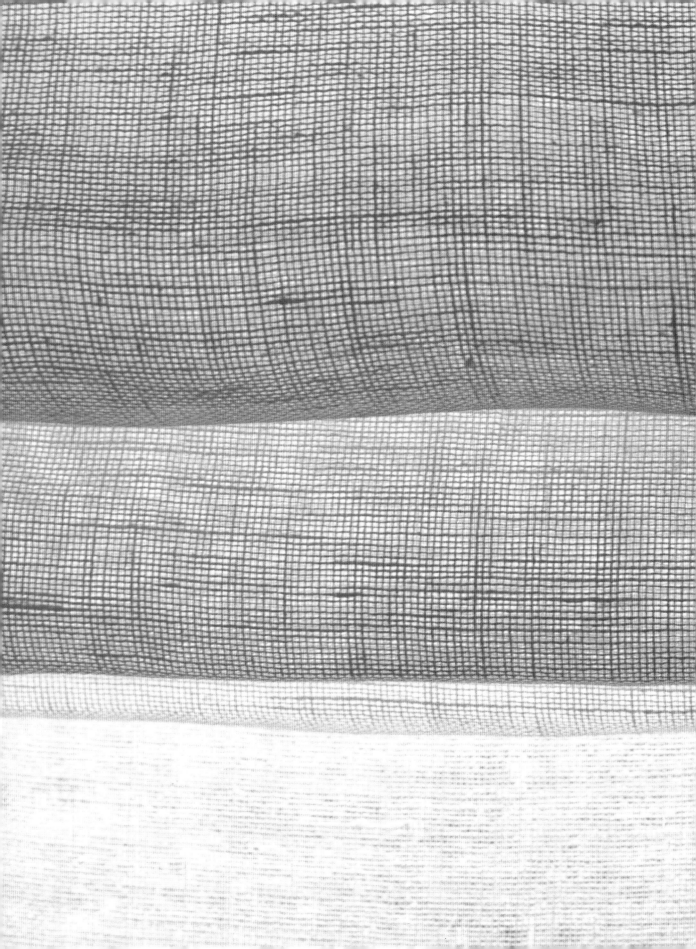

graphic roman blind

A loosely woven linen is good to use for an unlined Roman blind as it pleats well, always looks crisp and allows light into a room. Here the linen blind is finished with a deep grey felt border, which follows the outline of the window and adds some weight to the blind.

graphic roman blind

An unlined blind is a really useful window treatment where you need to admit light, need a bit of screening and don't want floor-length curtains. The pleats are best deep (about 35–50cm apart), and the dowels or rods should be as thin as possible. They are there to stop the fabric from sagging, but provide no support. This blind measures 90cm wide x 180cm drop, and the felt borders are 10cm wide all round.

Adjust the proportions to suit your window. Work out how many pleats you will have by dividing the drop into even spaces, each approximately 40cm deep.

I   To make the side borders, cut two long strips of felt 12cm wide by the drop of the blind plus 2cm seam allowance, plus a little extra for every pleat. This extra fabric will form the narrow pockets that hold the dowels and the measurement depends on the thickness of the rods: allow 2cm for a 0.5cm dowel or 4cm for a 1cm dowel. To make the top and bottom borders, cut two shorter strips, each 12cm wide by the width of the blind plus 2cm seam allowance.

2   Fold under and press a 1cm hem along each long side of the four border strips. Herringbone stitch them down (see p183).

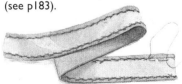

3   Lay a long strip wrong side up on a flat surface, and fold down the top right corner at a 45-degree angle, to meet the bottom edge. Press and open out. Repeat with the top left corner of a short strip. Using tailor's chalk and a ruler, draw a line on the wrong side of each strip to mark the creases.

4   Pin the two marked corners together with right sides facing, so that they lie edge to edge and the corners match precisely. Baste them together along the chalk lines. Machine stitch, working a few back stitches at both ends to secure the seam. Trim back the excess fabric, leaving an allowance of 0.5cm. Press the seam open and herringbone stitch down on each side. Repeat this

with the other two strips, then join all four to make a rectangular 'frame'.

5   Cut a piece of the linen the same size as the felt frame plus 1cm all round. Make a narrow double hem all round: turn under and press a 1.5cm turning along each side. Open out the fold, then turn in and press 0.5cm. If the linen is fine enough you shouldn't need to mitre the corners, but if they look at all bulky, neaten the excess fabric. To do this,

unfold both turnings and trim off the tip of the corner. Turn the corner in so that the four creases line up. Press lightly, then refold the double hem. Pin, baste and machine down all four sides.

6 Lay the linen over the felt frame, with wrong sides facing, leaving 0.5cm gap on all four sides. Pin and baste in position, then slip stitch by hand all round (see p 183). Turn over and slip stitch the inside edge of the frame to the linen.

7 To work out the spacing for the pockets, divide the length of the blind by the number of pleats required. Lay the blind wrong side up and mark each position with a pin at each side edge. Take both measurements from the top corners to ensure the lines are straight. Turn the top pleat over to the right side of the blind and press along the fold. Baste 1–2cm in from the fold (depending on the width of your dowels – see step 1), then machine stitch. This forms the first pocket. Open out and repeat for each pleat, then insert the dowels.

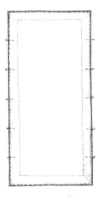

8 Sew two blind rings onto the back of every rod pocket, positioning one at each end, just inside the felt frame.

9 Cover the wooden batten with felt, using the staple gun. Make sure the corners are tucked under neatly.

10 Separate the two sides of the touch-and-close tape and hand sew the looped side to the wrong side of the blind 0.5cm from the top edge.

11 Staple the hooked side of the touch-and-close tape to the front edge of the batten. To attach and string the blind, follow the instructions on p179.

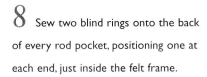

materials & equipment

Woven linen for centre panel

Felt for edging and batten

Touch-and-close tape, the width of the blind

Very thin dowels, the width of the blind, one for each pleat

Wooden batten, 5cm x 2.5cm, the width of the blind

2 screw eyes

Small metal or plastic blind rings, two for each pleat

Blind cord and acorn

Cleat with fixing screws

Staple gun

Ruler

Sewing kit

bands on tension wires

For lightweight curtains, tension wire used with metal eyelets has become a great modern method for hanging. Here panels have been created from finely woven linen alternated with a light 'parachute' cloth, sewn together with strips of drawn threadwork ribbon separating them. The eyelets allow the fabric to glide over the wire easily, and in summer the breeze through open windows lifts and moves the curtains to create a lovely billowing effect.

bands on tension wires

Eyelet kits are available from most good haberdashery departments and, with a little practice, are fairly easy to use. Always practise on scraps of the fabric that is to be used before you work on your final curtain. If you don't want to attach them yourself, there are companies that offer an eyeleting service (see suppliers, p189). In this project, the depths of the alternate strips of cloth have been chosen so that the more see-through linen is at eye level both for adults and children and the strips line up with the glazing bars. Work out the width of the panels according to the architecture of your windows. The drawn threadwork ribbon adds a tailored touch and cleverly hides the seams.

I   For all the pieces for one panel, except the top and bottom, cut strips of the two fabrics to the size required, plus 4cm extra in width and drop. Cut lengths of the ribbon the same width.

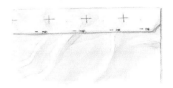

2   Lay the first strip right side down, then fold over 1cm along the top and bottom edges and press. Fold over a second time to make a double hem and press. Lay the top edge of a length of ribbon face down over the bottom edge. Pin, baste and machine down, close to the outside edge. Trim the remaining strips and join them as you go.

3   To make the top strip, cut a piece of fabric 4cm wider and 15cm longer than required. Cut a strip of buckram to the width of the finished panel. Fold and press a 7.5cm turning along the top edge of the fabric. Open out and lay the buckram into the crease so that it is centred on the strip. Fold in the top corners

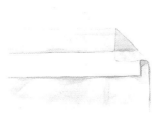

at a 45-degree angle, press them down, then fold over the top raw edge. Fold the buckram over, then pin, baste and machine down close to the inside edge.

4   On the wrong side of the fabric, mark the spacings for the eyelets, keeping them at least 1cm from the top and side edges. Insert the eyelets, following the instructions given with the kit.

5   Attach the top strip to the rest of the panel using the method given in step 2.

6   For the bottom strip, cut a piece of fabric 4cm wider and 16cm longer than required. Lay right side down and join the top to the bottom edge of the panel, as in step 2. Fold up and press a 16cm turning along the bottom. Open out and fold up 8cm to

meet the first crease, then fold up another 8cm. Press, pin and herringbone stitch down (see p183).

7 With the curtain right side down, turn in the sides 1cm twice to make a double hem. Mitre the corners if necessary. Press, pin and slip stitch down (see p183).

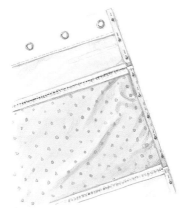

8 Install the tension wire as specified in the instructions. Thread the wire through the eyelets and tighten as necessary.

Make up the other panels in the same way.

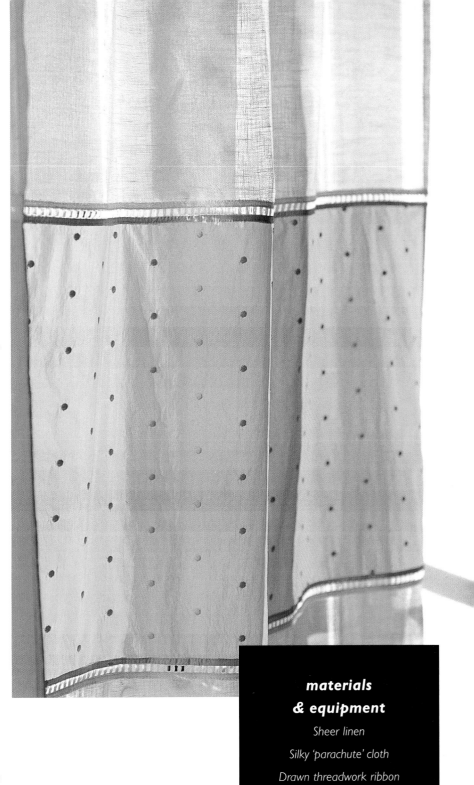

materials & equipment

Sheer linen

Silky 'parachute' cloth

Drawn threadwork ribbon

Buckram, 7.5cm wide

Eyelet kit

Tension wire kit

Sewing kit

mitred panel

With the more minimal look prevailing now, panels of fabric work well on windows, replacing fuller, fussier curtains. Here a heavy but loose woven cotton is bordered with a colourful stripe which is mitred on the corners. The panel is held up with an expansion pole which slips into a pocket at the back.

mitred panel

Expansion poles use tension to hold up curtains or panels and can be popped into a reveal in an instant. The key to this project is keeping the lines straight on the border. If you don't have a perfectly square window, it might be better to use a plain colour. Make sure your pocket is wide enough to hold your size of pole.

I   For the side borders, cut four long strips of striped fabric, the drop required plus 2.5cm, by the border width required plus 2.5cm. For the top and bottom borders, cut four shorter strips the same border width plus 2.5cm, by the width of the window plus 2.5cm. (The border here is 20cm wide.) Make certain that the stripes match up on each strip.

2   Lay one long strip wrong side down and place a short strip right side down over the top, aligning the two corners. Draw in a 45-degree angle from the top corner. Pin and baste the two strips together along this line, stopping 1.5cm from the bottom edge. Open out to check that the corner is square, then machine. Trim off the outside triangle of fabric and press the seam open. Add on another long and short strip to make a frame, then make a second frame from the remaining four strips.

3   To make the pocket for the expansion pole, cut a length of the striped fabric the width of the panel by the circumference of

the pole plus 5cm. Make sure the stripes run the length of the strip. You can also use plain fabric as an alternative. Turn in both short sides by 1cm, press and machine down. Fold the strip of fabric in half lengthways with right sides facing. Baste and machine along the long side, 1.5cm from the edge. Use a knitting needle to turn the tube right side out and press so the seam lies along one edge.

4   Lay one of the mitred frames on a flat surface, wrong side down. Pin the top of the pocket 0.5cm down from the top edge, then baste and machine. Baste and machine down the bottom edge of the pocket.

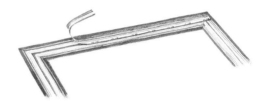

5   With right sides facing, place the two frames over each other. Pin, baste and machine together, 1cm from the outer edge. Clip the corners and trim away the excess fabric. Press in a 1.5cm hem to the wrong side along each raw inside edge of both frames. Turn the frame right side out and press.

6 Cut a panel of the loose woven fabric to the same size as the inside of the frame, plus 2cm all round. Insert the panel centrally between the two sides of the frame. Pin in place, then baste and machine together as close to the inside edge of the frame as possible.

7 Slip the expansion pole into the pocket and install the panel at the window.

double curtains

A pair of large glass doors open directly onto a beach, so curtains need to provide adequate privacy and shade in summer and warmth in winter. Double tracks are a good solution, with a tension wire to hold the sheer linen, and a stronger steel pole to hold the lined curtain. Frosted glass finials complete the cool effect.

There are a number of double-track systems available now, and this one is simple, elegant and strong (see credits, p187). The tension wire uses tiny opening clips while the front pole uses steel 'C' clips with a choice of two drops. The printed curtains are lined, and edged in a wide grosgrain ribbon. The heading is made using two small channels about 10cm apart through which piping cord can be threaded and then gathered up. Metal curtain hooks are handsewn to the back. A pair of ties is sewn above each hook for decoration rather than practical use, although you could use them instead of the hooks.

I   For one inner curtain, cut one and a half widths of the sheer fabric for the drop required plus 7.5cm. Join the widths using a French seam (see p102, step 1). Press, baste and machine stitch a 2.5cm double hem around three sides, then attach narrow heading tape following the instructions on p182.

double curtains

2   For one outer lined curtain, cut two drops of fabric the length required plus 31cm, remembering to include enough for pattern repeats (see p179). Cut two drops of lining the length you need plus 4cm. Cut enough regular piping cord for twice the width of the curtain.

3   Pin the two widths of fabric rights sides together, baste, machine stitch a 1.5cm seam and press open. Snip the selvedges.

4   Pin 6cm turnings on either side, baste and slip stitch (see p183) them to the wrong side of the fabric. Press.

5   Fold down the top of the curtain 11cm, press and open out. Fold up the bottom 20cm. Press, open out and fold in the raw edge to meet the crease. Press and open out.

6   Cut a piece of the grosgrain ribbon the finished drop of the curtain plus 15cm. With the curtain wrong side down, pin the ribbon to the leading edge of the curtain, starting 6cm from the top and ending 10cm from the bottom. Baste and machine down both edges of the ribbon. On the wrong side, turn up the bottom to make a double 10cm hem and herringbone stitch (see p183) to secure. Hand sew the two open edges.

7   Cut a piece of grosgrain ribbon to the finished width of the curtain plus 3cm. Pin and baste the ribbon along the bottom edge of the curtain, folding under on the diagonal at the corner to make a

mitre where it meets the ribbon and finishing flush on the other side. Machine in place. Trim back the ribbon.

8   Overlock the top edges of the lining widths. With rights sides together, join them as for the curtain; they now need to be the same width as the curtain. Cut to the size if necessary and overlock the edges.

9   Fold and press up a 12cm hem turning. Open out, fold and press in 6cm. Fold in again and pin, baste and machine the hem along its top edge. Turn in the lining sides by 3cm. Pin, baste and slip stitch in place.

10   Place the lining wrong side down over the main fabric right side down. It should lie 3cm in from the edges on either side and both sets of turnings should be in alignment. The lining hem should be 3cm higher than the fabric hem. Pin, baste and slip stitch the lining to the curtain on both sides.

11   Press a turning of 2cm along the top of the curtain, turn down a further 9cm using the crease made in step 5 as a guide. Press down, enclosing the top of the lining.

12   Pin and baste the ribbon to the top of the turning on the wrong side so that barely 1cm will show on the right side, and machine 0.5cm from the top, enclosing the raw edges of the ribbon.

13 Lay piping cord below this seam from one side of the curtain to the other, between the two layers of fabric. Pin and baste it into position. Machine a second row creating a channel of 1cm enclosing the cord. Make a second channel in the same way 6cm below the first. The rows of stitches will secure the turning, the hem and the lining.

14 Secure the piping cords at one end with stab stitches and pull the cord through until the required width is arrived at. Secure this end in the same way and arrange the gathers evenly.

15 On the wrong side and starting 2cm in from the edge, mark the positions for and sew on nine equally spaced brass curtain hooks. The tops of the hooks should be level with the top row of stitches.

16 For the ties, cut nine lengths of the thicker piping cord 90cm long. Cut on the bias nine pieces of fabric 90 x 3cm. Sew the long sides right sides together. Using a knitting needle, turn right sides out.

17 Bind the end of a piece of piping cord, attach it to a safety pin and feed it back through the tie. Knot the ends to neaten, snip the end and stitch each tie at its halfway mark over the top of each hook.

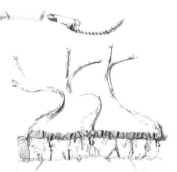

Repeat for the other curtain, bearing in mind the position of the pattern repeats and the side to which the ribbon is to be attached.

materials
& equipment
Linen for outer curtains
Lining
Sheer fabric for inner curtain
Grosgrain ribbon
Regular piping cord for curtains
Thicker piping cord for ties
Brass curtain hooks
Double track system
Transparent heading tape
Knitting needle
Safety pin
Ruler
Sewing kit

appliqué valance

There is often a need to hide the headings of curtains and traditionally this has been done using elaborate pelmet boards and on stiff valances. But in a more contemporary setting these methods look cumbersome and fussy, and have a tendency to cut out a lot of light. In this case a wonderful river view wanted very little interference, yet the tops of the curtains and tracks needed hiding. The solution is a very narrow soft valance with an appliqué wave in a contrasting colour.

appliqué valance

The curtains were made using 3m wide fabric and so I was able to make one continuous curtain with no drop joins. There was enough left over to use for the valance. If you can't find wide fabric, join drops as necessary. To make a basic unlined curtain see p58. The valance is attached with brackets that clip on to the front of the curtain track. It is lined with a heavy interlining to make a smoother curve on this long expanse of window.

1 For the valance, cut a piece of the curtain fabric the width required plus 4cm and twice the drop plus 6cm. Fold in half lengthways, right side facing out and press. Open out. Fold down the top 3cm right side facing out, press and open out.

2 Following the finished project as a guide, make a template by drawing a repeat of a shallow wave pattern on paper, slightly narrower than the finished valance.

3 Cut a strip of the contrast fabric the width required plus 4cm and at least 4cm wider than the widest part of the template. With the fabric facing down, pin the paper template to one end of the fabric and outline with tailor's chalk. Remove and move the template along, repeating until you have completed the width of the strip. Cut out the fabric 1cm outside the chalk marks along the top and bottom lines.

4 With the wavy strip facing wrong side down, machine along both long edges following the chalked lines. Snip the 1cm turning

allowance every 5cm or so, almost to the stitch line. Fold in and baste on both sides and lay over the opened-out strip from step 1, centring it half way between the two crease lines with a 3cm seam allowance at the top. Pin, baste, and machine.

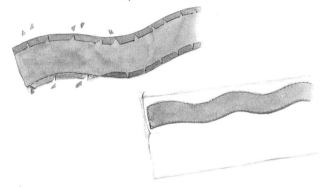

5 Cut a strip of interlining the width of the finished valance required by the drop plus 3cm. Lay the appliquéd piece of cloth right side down on a flat surface, and lay the interlining along the middle crease line, and centred on both sides. Catch the interlining to the crease using lock stitch (see p184).

6 Fold in the sides by 2cm, press and open out. Fold this in half, press and fold in again to make a double hem. Hand stitch catching only a very few threads to the interlining.

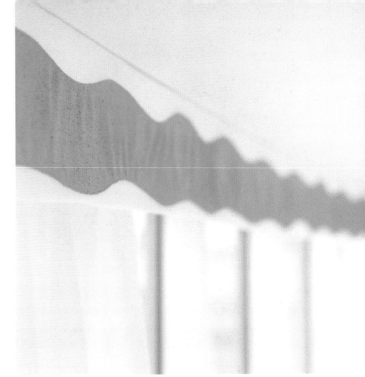

7 Fold up the fabric over the interlining. Pin, then baste a line 3cm from the top. Turn the fabric over. Cut a length of the touch-and-close tape the width required and pin the looped side along the basted thread line. Baste and machine along this line only. Remove all the basting, turn the fabric over again and trim away the excess fabric and interlining behind the tape.

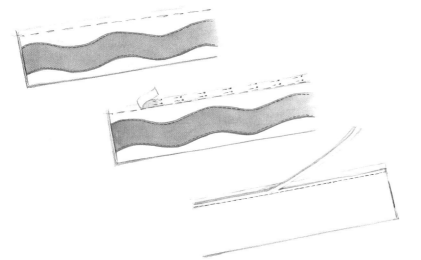

8 With the right side facing down, turn down the touch-and-close tape and hand stitch catching only the back layer of fabric. Attach the hooked side of the touch-and-close tape to the track and hang the valance.

materials & equipment

Curtain fabric with enough left over for valance
Contrast fabric for appliqué
Paper for template
Heavy interlining
20mm wide adhesive touch-and-close tape, the width of the valance
Sewing kit

swedish blind

This type of blind is used all over Sweden in lieu of curtains: a tribute to double glazing and good insulation! A minimal window covering, this works best using a weighty reversible woven linen that falls comfortably. The special glass rings allow the cord to glide smoothly.

swedish blind

Easy to make and easy to use. The blind is attached with touch-and-close tape to a wooden batten which, in turn, is screwed either to the ceiling above a window or over the top of the window. In this instance, I used a double layer of linen for added insulation, and made it like a bag.

I Cut two pieces of linen 15cm longer than the drop required and 4cm wider than the finished blind. Lay the pieces on a flat surface, right sides facing. Pin together the two sides and the bottom, then baste and machine stitch 2cm in from the edge. Clip the corners and trim away the excess fabric from the seams, then overlock or zigzag the raw edges. Turn right side out and press.

2 Lay the blind on a flat surface. Press and baste down a 2cm turning along the top. Pin the looped side of the touch-and-close tape to the blind so that it covers the raw edges. Baste and machine down.

3 Staple the bottom of the blind to the dowel rod.

4 Using the staple gun, cover the batten with a strip of linen, folding the corners neatly. Staple the hooked strip of touch-and-close tape to the front side of the batten.

5 To make the tabs, cut two pieces of linen, each 30cm by 10cm. Fold each in half lengthways with right sides facing. Pin together along the long edge, then baste and machine leaving a 0.5cm seam allowance. Turn right side out and press. Fold in half, slip a tab onto each glass ring and staple the raw ends of the tabs to the back of the batten.

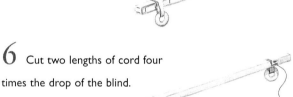

6 Cut two lengths of cord four times the drop of the blind. Tie a knot at one end of each piece, then staple the knots to the batten over the ends of the tabs.

7 Using a bradawl, make two holes in the front of the batten, piercing the touch-and-close tape so that it will not be twisted. Drill through the wood and screw the batten into the window recess. Fix the cleat to the side of the window.

8 Fix the blind to the batten with the touch-and-close tape and string it according to the diagram. Roll the fabric to the front before drawing up fully.

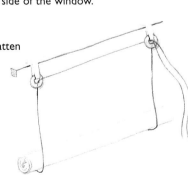

A very ordinary window, which sits rather uncomfortably high from the floor, is transformed with a minimal treatment. Translucent scrim panels allow light to flood into the room, while extra button-on panels provide privacy. Linen squares at the centre of each buttoned panel are embroidered to provide distinctive detail.

layered linen panels

layered linen panels

This is a good solution for a difficult window, where privacy and light are both needed. These scrim panels, which allow light in yet obscure the view, have buttoned on panels of linen, some with monograms blanket-stitched to them and others plain.

I Cut pieces of scrim to the size required plus 2cm extra all round. Turn the sides under 2cm and press. Open out and press in 1cm to make a double hem, then unfold all the creases. Trim and mitre the corners, then refold the hems. Slip stitch (see p183) the mitres, and machine down the four sides.

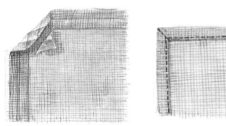

3 Mark the positions of the buttonholes on the linen and work them by hand or machine. Lay the linen back over the scrim panels and mark with pins where the buttons are to be sewn. Sew the buttons to the scrim.

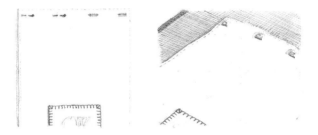

2 To make the button-on panels, cut pieces of linen to the size required plus 1cm all round. Turn in 0.5cm twice on all sides to make a narrow double hem, then press, baste and machine. Cut out the monogram and press in 0.5cm on all four sides. Pin to the centre of the linen panel, right sides up, and baste. Blanket stitch in place using the blue embroidery thread.

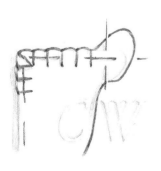

4 Cut two 5cm lengths of cotton tape, double over to make hanging loops and hand stitch to the back of the scrim panels, just below the top at the hemmed sides.

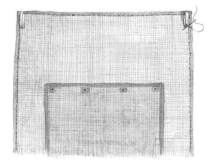

5 To hang the panels, attach screws into the window frame, in line with the hanging loops. Hang the scrim panels. Dab glue onto each screw head and stick the pebbles in place.

Crisp, fresh and utilitarian: tea towels sewn into a patchwork pattern can make a sophisticated pair of curtains. Coupled with the grand chandelier and the huge scale of the room, the humble tea towel adds a wonderful touch of humour.

patchwork curtains

patchwork curtains

These curtains have a drop of about 3m, with double fullness in each curtain. To work out how many tea towels you will need, measure out the width and drop of your curtain on the floor, and organize your selection of towels into a satisfactory pattern. If you have gaps anywhere, these can be filled with patches of plain white tea towels. Then make sure you have two of each towel so that the pattern of the second curtain will mirror the first to make an exact pair.

I   Starting from the top of the curtain, lay the tea towels wrong side up on the floor, overlapping the edges by about 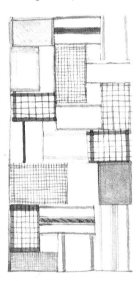 1.5cm. If all your tea towels are the same size, lay them out in rows to form a brick-wall pattern. If not, use the plain white ones to cover up any gaps that form between them. Pay particular attention to the leading edge of the curtain, as visually this is the most important area. Include a minimum of 17cm extra in the drop and 10cm extra in the width for hems.

2   Start joining the tea towels from the top edge downwards. Pin the first two together with right sides facing, leaving a seam allowance of about 1cm. Baste, then machine stitch. Open out the seam and press. Continue joining the towels, as if assembling a jigsaw, stitching and pressing as you go.

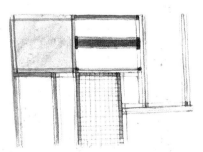

3   To make the heading, lay the stitched jigsaw of fabrics wrong side up and place a strip of 5cm wide buckram across the top, leaving a margin of 5cm at each side of the curtain and 2.5cm along the top edge.

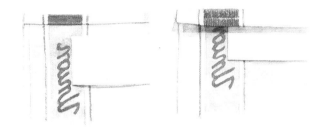

Fold the top 2.5cm down over the buckram and press. Fold down the buckram and press.

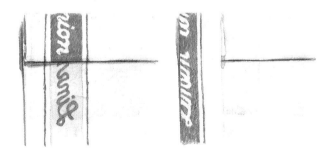

4   Turn in and press a 5cm fold along the side, open out and press in half. Refold to make a double hem. Herringbone stitch (see p183) the side hems down to 10cm from the bottom of the curtain, then herringbone stitch the top to secure the buckram.

5   Make a double hem along the bottom edge. Press up a 5cm turning, then open out, and press in half. Secure two curtain

weights to the inside corners. Turn the original fold back up and herringbone stitch by hand. Finish the corners with neat stitches.

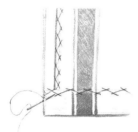

6 Cut and join two drops of lining the same width as the hemmed curtain plus 4cm, and the same drop as the curtain plus 6cm. Turn in and press a 2.5cm hem along the side and top edges, then machine down. Turn up a 4cm hem along the bottom edge, press and machine down. Lay the hemmed lining over the curtain with wrong sides facing, centred on the sides, and just barely above the bottom hem. Pin, baste and slip stitch (see p183) along the side and top edges, leaving the bottom open. Press.

Make the second curtain in the same way, reversing the arrangement of the tea towels. Hang the curtains in place using curtain clips, spaced about 15–20cm apart.

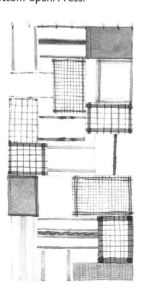

materials & equipment

Approx. 40 blue and white tea towels, washed and pressed, with any hems neatly trimmed away

Extra plain white tea towels for patches

Lining

Buckram, 5cm wide, the width of the ungathered curtains

8 curtain weights

Curtain clips

Sewing kit

Miniature portière rods were specially commissioned to hold this panel of cutwork cotton. Fitted both top and bottom, it swings easily to open and close. The opaque cotton gives a lovely translucent light to the room while maintaining privacy. This type of fitting is also useful on French doors and windows.

portière panel

portière panel

Portière rods are easily available from curtain fixture manufacturers. However, these very thin ones were specially made by an ironmonger. As an alternative, you could use net curtain suspension wire. The fabric is attached using narrow pockets, and here the key is accuracy. The panel needs to be taut or it will flap like a sail, and a little fabric stiffener will give a crisper effect, if necessary.

I   First measure or calculate the circumference of the rods, which in this case was 5cm. To this amount add 1cm for the upstand and 1cm for seaming, arriving at an 7cm allowance per pocket. To calculate the drop of the panel, add the pocket measurement x 2 to the distance between the rods. For the width, add 3cm for hemming.

2   With the fabric right side down, fold in the sides by 3cm and press. Open this out, then fold and press in a 1.5cm turning so that the raw edge lines up exactly with the first crease. Baste and machine stitch down.

3   With the panel right side down, fold up the bottom by the pocket measurement (in this case 7cm) and press. Open it out and fold the turning in half so that the raw edge lines up with the crease. Fold again to make a deep double hem, then pin and baste. Machine down close to the edge. Using a ruler and a pencil or tailor's chalk, measure and draw a line 1cm from the bottom edge. Machine along this line to make the upstand.

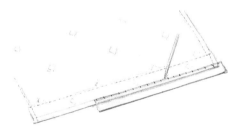

4   Turn the fabric the other way up and repeat step 3 to make the top pocket. Fix the rods to the window and slot the pockets over them to fix the panel in place.

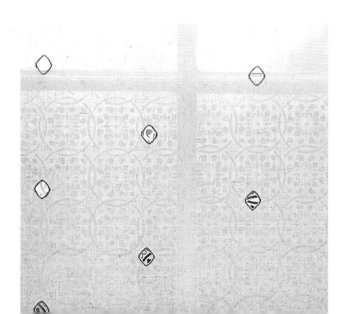

materials
& equipment

White broderie anglaise fabric

2 portière rods

Long ruler and pencil

Screwdriver

Sewing kit

sliding panels

Tailored layers of sheer voile and heavy linen on a sliding panel system look streamlined and provide multi-functional use. The patterned voile diffuses the strong reflected light, and the linen provides total privacy from the outside.

sliding panels

For a sleek and modern window treatment this weighted sliding panel system is hard to beat. It is made up of four separate tracks within a casing, and in each track there are one or two panels of fabric which are weighted at the bottom and attached at the top with touch-and-close tape. They can be individually moved to provide versatility and maximum light control. There are a mixture of opaque and translucent sheer panels that can be manoeuvred around to give total privacy or just screen the sun, or a mixture of the two. This system is available made to measure, and you can vary the number of tracks and panels. For suppliers, see credits p187.

I   Cut the required amount of panels from each fabric, 3cm wider and 7cm longer than the finished size.

2   Lay a panel wrong side up on a flat surface and turn in both sides 1.5cm. Press, open out and fold in half. Press in and refold along the first crease to form a double hem. Pin, baste and machine stitch down both sides.

3   Turn down the top 1cm and press. Cut a length of the looped side of the touch-and-close tape the exact width of the panel and lay over the top, covering the raw edge of the fabric. Pin, baste and machine down.

4   Turn up the bottom 3cm and press. Turn up a further 3cm and press. Open out both folds. Lay the weighted bar between the two crease lines, centred on both sides. Turn up the fabric twice and pin. Take out the bar. Baste and machine close to the edge of the fold and feed the bar back in, centring it. Close the two open ends by hand to keep the bar in place. Make the remaining panels in the same way.

5   Install the panel glide system according to the manufacturer's instructions.

**materials
& equipment**

White opaque linen

Sheer fabric

Touch-and-close tape

*Panel glide track system which
will include the tracks, the
weighted bars and panel carriers
(see credits p187)*

Sewing kit

Comfort, elegance and timelessness are the key elements of a classic interior: the feeling when you walk into a room that all is well, the proportions are correct, the colours don't jar, the furniture is comfortable yet stylish, and the window treatments enhance the room. The projects in this chapter are full of tactile fabrics – scrunchy taffeta, thirsty terry cloth, and warm wool – and the classic style is evoked as much through their textures as through the treatment. The designs range from formal Italian-strung taffeta curtains to a simple roller blind made from traditional mattress ticking, and each one is sensitive to the architecture of its window and the requirements of the owner. Proportion plays a big role with classic curtains: floor-length curtains need enough fullness to drape well, but not so much as to look messy; a self-valance curtain needs a deep enough drop in relation to the window. As always, the colour and detail, such as the addition of a velvet trim, are what makes a treatment successful.

classic

The window treatments illustrated on these pages embody the classic

style. The projects, which begin overleaf, offer various interpretations of

the look for the modern home.

terry shower curtain

A cast iron, roll-top bath looks majestic with this terry cloth shower curtain, which is attached to a chrome ring with large metal eyelets and hooks. The edges are finished in a crisp cotton trimming braid, and the terry cloth is lined in a sheer synthetic fabric that repels moisture. The curtain drapes generously onto the floor for a sumptuous feel.

terry shower curtain

Huge metal eyelets can be obtained from specialist suppliers (see credits, p187) and require a level of skill and strength to fit. However, more and more curtain makers and curtain hardware manufacturers offer an eyeleting service (see suppliers, p188), which is probably the most economical way to make sure that you end up with an accurate row of eyelets. As the top of this curtain needed to be firm enough to 'stand up', we used fairly heavyweight buckram to stiffen it. You need a deceptively large amount of material for this design, as the fabric needs to fan out over the width and depth of the bath. Measure and calculate carefully before you begin.

I   Cut three drops of each fabric, the length required plus 52cm. Remember that the width of the tub takes up a lot of drop, so allow plenty. Join the widths of terry cloth and lining (see p181).

2   Place the terry cloth on a flat surface, wrong side down. Lay the lining over the top, right side down so that all four edges match up. Pin, then baste and machine stitch around the top and two sides. Clip the corners and turn right side out.

3   With the terry cloth right side down, lay the curtain out flat and fold the top down 15cm. Press and open out. Place the buckram strip below the crease line, leaving a 3cm gap at each side. Pin in place.

4   Press a 3cm turning along both sides of the curtain. Pin, baste and machine down over the buckram.

5   Fold the top edge down over the buckram, then fold the buckram back over itself. Pin in place and slip stitch (see p183).

6   Using the tool provided with the kit, fix a row of eyelets along the centre of the buckram, approximately 30cm apart.

7   To hem the bottom, press a 20cm turning along the bottom edge. Open it out, fold up and press a 10cm turning so that the raw edge lines up with the crease. Refold, then pin, baste and slip stitch closed.

8   Hand sew the cotton braid along the top and bottom edges and down both sides. Insert a metal hook through each eyelet and loop over the shower ring.

materials
& equipment

Terry cloth,
at least three times the
circumference of the shower ring
Transparent waterproof fabric for
lining, same width as terry cloth
Cotton braid
Buckram, 15cm wide and 5cm
shorter than the width of the
curtain
Eyelet kit
Metal hooks
Sewing kit

fringed roller blind

In a tight space like this tiny bathroom, a spring roller blind is a good solution. It takes up very little space yet looks decorative. Roller blind kits can work with almost any fabric so you can coordinate a scheme, and only a small amount of fabric is required. The cotton bobble fringe adds a little fun and humour.

I   Roller blind kits are readily available. Follow the manufacturer's instructions for making; then just before installing, finish off the bottom edge by hand stitching a length of fringe and gluing a length of velvet ribbon with fabric glue just above the wooden dowel.
Install according to the instructions.

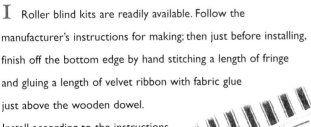

edged wool curtains

A country farmhouse with rough plastered walls and a cosy wood-burning stove has a low casement window hung with rich cream wool curtains. The heavy wool is unlined, providing enough warmth for the winter, but admitting diffused sunlight in summer. The curtains are hung with simple wooden rings on an antique pole and are edged with a band of large scallops and a wool bobble fringe.

edged wool curtains

There are so many wonderful heavy fabrics on the market now that are finished on both sides and need no lining that curtain-making can be really easy. The scallops have been backed with iron-on interling to keep them pert and cut with pinking shears to prevent fraying.

1   Cut three lengths of fabric the drop required plus 27cm for hem and turnings. For one curtain, cut one piece in half lengthways and, with right sides facing, pin, baste and machine one half width to one width along the selvedges. Press the seams flat.

2   The scalloped edging is made from a narrow strip of the fabric. To work out the length, take 6cm for the heading and seams away from the final drop and divide by the number of scallops. As a guide, fourteen scallops with a 15cm diameter will fit along a 213cm drop. Calculate the width by adding 4cm plus a seam allowance of 1.5cm to the radius of the scallop. Cut the strip from the side of the half width. Iron a length of interfacing to the wrong side of the fabric and overlock the long edge.

3   Make a circular card template the same size as the finished scallop and draw on the diameter. Place the strip of fabric right side down on a flat surface with the interfacing facing upwards and using tailor's chalk, mark a line a radius width

from the raw edge. Using the diameter line on the template as a guide, draw in the semi-circular scallops and cut them out with pinking shears, following the curves exactly.

4   Overlock all four edges of the curtain. With the wrong side facing downwards and starting 6cm down from the top, pin the bobble braid along the leading edge so that the bobbles only will show out from a 1.5cm seam. The braid should finish 24cm up from the bottom corner.

5   With right sides facing, lay the scalloped strip right side down over the braid, so that the bobbles are sandwiched between the two layers. Pin, baste and machine it in place.

6   Turn up a 24cm hem on the right side of the curtain. Pin and baste the side edges together and machine stitch leaving a 1.5cm seam allowance. Clip the corners and turn right sides out so that the hem now lies on the wrong side. Pin, baste and slip stitch (see p183) the hem in place. Press under a 1.5cm hem along the unfinished side and machine down.

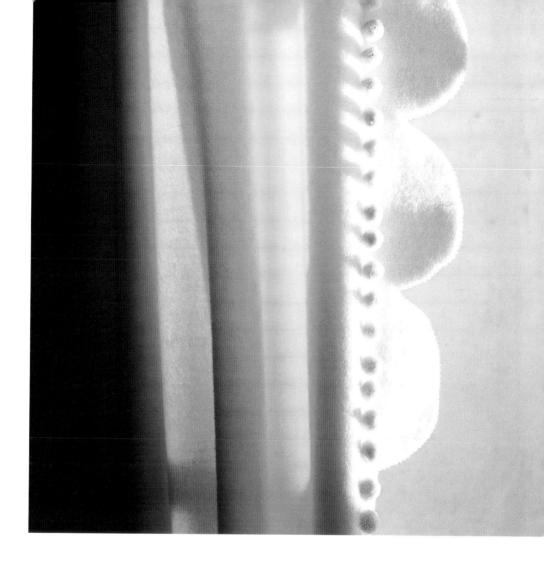

7   Turn down the overlocked tops by 3cm and slip stitch them together. Cut a length of heading tape the same length as the top edge and press under 1cm at each end. Pin in place, then baste and machine in place.

Make the second curtain in the same way, reversing the leading edge to make a matching pair.

materials
& equipment

Loosely woven cream
wool fabric
Iron-on interfacing
Bobble braid
Narrow heading tape
Pinking shears
Card for template
Pair of compasses
Long ruler
Sewing kit

unlined curtains with ribbon trim

In a large bay window heavy, cream, roughly woven linen drapes elegantly to the floor. Wide bands of fuchsia velvet and mauve satin ribbon are hand sewn to make a border.

unlined curtains with ribbon trim

Handmade curtain headings require very accurate sewing skills and a lot of time and patience. The reward is curtains that look like couture-made clothes: no stitch lines anywhere, and a wonderful flow of fabric. These curtains are made from the most sumptuous and heavily woven thick linen. Because they hang in a bay window, lining and interlining would have added to the bulk, made the stack back too wide and cut out the light. Each curtain has two full widths.

I Cut two drops of the linen, the drop required plus 22cm. As these curtains won't be lined, the drops are joined with a French seam, which encloses the raw edges and prevents fraying. Pin and baste the two pieces of linen together, long edges matching and wrong sides facing. Machine stitch 1cm from the edge and secure the ends of the seam by backstitching with the machine. Trim back the selvedges to 0.5cm. Turn the fabric right sides together and press so that the machined line is right at the edge. Baste, then machine 1cm from the edge. Open out and press the seam to one side. Overlock the sides.

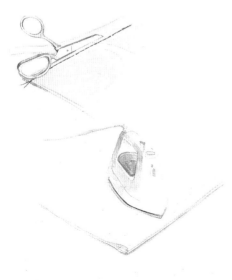

2 Press in a 5cm single hem along each side. Turn up the bottom to make a double 5cm hem by first ironing in a crease 10cm up from the lower edge. Open out and fold in a 5cm crease so the raw edge lines up exactly with the first crease. Press. Refold the first crease and herringbone stitch the hem in place (see p183). Hand close the open ends with small stitches.

3 Turn down the top 2cm and press, then open out the fold. Open out the side hems. Place the strip of buckram

along the top crease so that the short ends line up with the side creases. Turn in the corners at a 45-degree angle, then refold the side and top hems to make mitres. Slip stitch (see p183) the mitres. Herringbone the top edge to the buckram. Slip stitch the side hems.

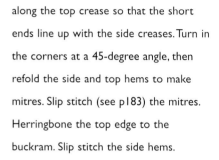

4 Turn down the buckram and herringbone stitch. Hand stitch the open ends neatly. Using the strong thread, sew two parallel lines of long running stitches into the buckram (see p183). The top row should be 1.5cm from the top, and the bottom row 7cm further down. Make

certain that the stitches in both rows are the same length and lined up exactly. Pull up the two threads and gather up to the required width. Knot off securely.

5 Cut a piece of linen 8cm wide by the finished width of the curtain, plus 4cm for turnings. Place on a flat surface, wrong side up. Baste the webbing strip along the centre and press in the corners to mitre. Press the two long edges over to cover the webbing and stitch down. Turn in the mitres and slip stitch in place. Lay the curtain on a flat surface, wrong side up. Place the strip of covered webbing, right side up, over the gathered pleats 1.5cm from the top edge. Pin, baste, then hand stitch it firmly to the pleats, taking in both the fabric and the buckram.

6 Firmly sew the pin hooks to the strip of covered webbing at regular intervals of 15–20cm.

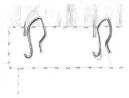

Make the second curtain in the same way, then hang at the window.

7 Pin and baste the first wide band of ribbon approximately 20cm from the bottom edge, wrapping a small amount round to the back, and slip stitch in place. Attach the other ribbon to the curtain in the same way, 5cm further up.

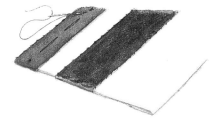

materials
& equipment
Heavily woven linen
Ribbons for trimming
Thin buckram, 10cm wide, the
width of the ungathered curtains
Webbing tape 3cm wide, the
width of the finished curtains
Strong sewing thread
Pin hooks
Sewing kit

contrast lined curtains

Tall and elegant Georgian windows look graceful with ivory linen curtains that are
lined in a black and ivory classical print, echoing the monochromatic colours of the
room. The plain, thin, wrought iron poles, to which the curtains are tied, are
simplicity itself. Ties make it possible for the curtains to be reversed.

contrast lined curtains

Lining plain curtains with a pattern can be subtle and surprising. These are lined in a classic toile de Jouy print, which is outlined with the addition of a black rolled piping cord. It is advisable to use a layer of interlining so that the pattern is not visible from the plain side.

I Cut a drop of the main fabric, the length required plus 10cm. Cut a drop of interlining to the same size. Place the main fabric, wrong side up, on a flat surface. Lay the interlining on top,

matching the edges exactly. Turn back one half of the interlining width ways and lock stitch it (see p184) to the main fabric along the fold. Lay the interlining flat again.

2 Fold in 5cm on all four sides, taking in both the fabric and the interlining and treating them as one. Press the hems in place, then open them out. Mitre the corners: turn each one in at a 45-degree angle, aligning the creases. Press, then refold the hems. Trim away the excess triangles of interlining if the corners look too bulky, then slip stitch (see p183) the mitres in place. Slip stitch down the side hems and herringbone stitch (see p183) the top and bottom hems.

3 Cut out a drop of the contrast lining the same size as the hemmed curtain. Lay it on a flat surface with the wrong side facing upwards. Turn in and press a 2.5cm hem along each side. Mitre and slip stitch the corners, then slip stitch the vertical hems and herringbone stitch the horizontal hems as before.

4 To make the ties, cut five strips of the main fabric, each 8cm wide and 40cm long. With the right side facing down, turn in the two long sides by 2cm. Press. Open out and fold in half to meet the first crease. Press and open out. Repeat for the two short sides. Trim off the outside triangles and fold in the corners at a 45-degree angle across the inner corners. Fold in the long sides twice, then the short sides twice. Pin, baste and machine stitch close to the edge.

5 Lay the interlined curtain, wrong side up, on a flat surface. Divide the top edge into four equal sections and mark the divisions with pins. Fold the ties in half, right side out. Pin and baste a tie at each mark, so that the folded edges are 3cm down from the top. Machine each tie in place.

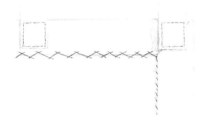

6 Place the hemmed lining over the curtain right side up, leaving a 2.5cm gap all round, then pin and baste it in place. Slip stitch together on all four sides.

7 Cut a length of satin piping to fit around the edge of the curtain plus 5cm. Hand stitch the black trim all round to cover the join.

Make the second curtain in the same way, matching the fabric drops carefully, then hang at the window.

materials & equipment

Main fabric, including
enough for ties
Contrast lining fabric
Black rolled satin piping cord
Interlining
Sewing kit

shaped roller blind

Roller blinds are universally used for window coverings and are easily available in kit form. They can look a little boring so why not modify them to suit a room? As long as you follow the instructions for making the blind very carefully, and for installing it, a few changes to the bottom are easy. To this one I have added a decorative band of scallops which are edged in a smart black velvet piping.

Make the basic blind to the size you require, following the manufacturer's instructions and cutting the pole and lath to length. Finish off the bottom edge by hand stitching a length of fringing or, for a more decorative effect, add a scalloped border before attaching the blind to the pole and mounting.

I   To make the edging, cut a piece of fabric the same width as the blind plus 2cm seam allowance and twice the depth of the scallops (about 20cm) plus 2cm. Make sure the stripes line up with those on the blind. Fold the fabric in half, wrong sides together, and press. Turn under 1cm at both ends and press. Divide the width of the blind by the number of scallops you require and cut out a circle of card with this diameter. Draw a line across the centre of the circle.

2   Place the template at one corner of the folded edge so that the line is parallel to the fold. Using a ruler and a soft pencil or tailor's chalk, draw a straight line across the fabric, in line with the diameter. Draw around the template for each scallop, matching the diameter up to the chalk line each time.

3   Pin the two sides of the fabric together at the centre of each semi-circle to prevent slippage. Using a pair of sharp scissors, cut out the scallops.

4   Lay one piece of fabric right side up and pin and baste the piping selvedge along the scallops and the two sides, matching the raw edges.

5   Place the second piece of fabric over the top, right side down, so that the scallops match up and the piping is sandwiched between the two layers. Pin, baste and machine stitch all around the scallops and

two sides, taking in the piping. Use a zipper foot to stitch close to the piping cord, making sure that it lies on the inside of the stitching.

6 Trim the excess fabric from the seams. Clip the curves and in between the scallops so that the fabric will lie flat.

7 Turn right sides out and press. Pin, baste and machine the scalloped edge to the bottom edge of the blind and snip off the piping level with the blind.

8 Hand sew the beads in the spaces between the scallops, and the tassel between the two central scallops.

materials & equipment

Roller blind kit

Fabric with a very close weave plus extra fabric for the scallops

Contrast piping for scallops

Beads

Tassel

Pair of compasses

Thin card for template

Long ruler

Sewing kit

self-valance curtains

A tall, narrow window takes on a better proportion with the addition of a fringed
valance on each curtain to avoid cutting out too much light. Using the stripe
horizontally for the valance gives the illusion of widening the window.

self-valance curtains

A self-valance is a useful decorating trick in many situations. It obviates the need for a fussy pelmet or complete valance yet gives a decorative effect and can help solve proportion problems. Both the curtains and the valances are lined; the curtain has double fullness and each valance is cut to the exact width of the finished curtain.

I Cut a single width of fabric the drop required plus 12.5cm. Lay the fabric on a flat surface with the right side facing upwards. Starting at the top corner of the leading edge, pin and baste a length of fringe so that just the triangles of the fringe will show when a 1.5cm seam has been stitched. Finish 10cm short of the bottom corner.

2 Cut a piece of lining the same width and drop as the main fabric. Place, right side downwards, over the main fabric and fringe. Pin and baste the sides together and machine stitch 1.5cm seams. You now have a bag. Press in 1cm all around the bottom edge, then turn up a 10cm hem. Pin, baste and machine in place. Turn the curtain right sides out and press.

3 For the valance, cut a piece with the stripes running horizontally, the drop required by the finished width required, plus 3cm for turnings. Cut a piece of lining the same size. Cut a length of fringe to the same drop. With the fabric right side upwards, attach the fringe to one short side so that just the triangles of the fringe will project beyond the seam line of 1.5cm. Place the lining on top, right side down. Pin, baste and machine the sides and bottom. Turn right sides out and press.

4 Pin and baste the top raw edges of the curtain and its lining together. Measuring carefully, pin ten pleats at regular intervals along the top edge so that the total width of the curtain equals that of the valance. Baste down and machine in place 1cm from the top.

5 With the fabric side of the valance facing the lining side of the curtain pleats, pin the two together along the raw edges.

Machine together, then overlock the seam. Turn over and oversew the valance and curtain edges together 2cm from this seam.

6 Sew ten curtain rings at equal intervals along the top of the seam using buttonhole thread. Mark fifteen regularly spaced points along the bottom of the valance and sew a tassel securely to each one.

Make the second curtain in the same way, remembering to keep the fringe on the leading edge.

materials & equipment

Striped fabric

Plain lining fabric, the same width

Triangular hessian fringe

30 string tassels

20 large curtain rings

Buttonhole thread

Sewing kit

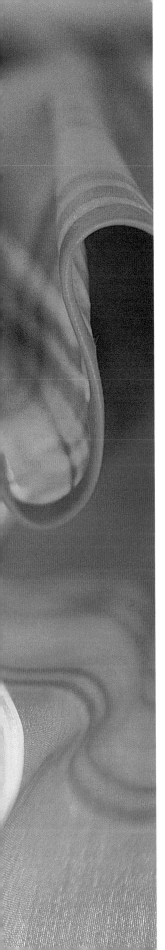

fixed taffeta curtains

Unlined plaid silk taffeta curtains have fixed headings but can be opened using a system of rings sewn in a diagonal line, with string threaded through them, called Italian stringing. It works well on silk and lightweight fabrics that can billow. The heading is hidden by a gathered short valance attached to a wooden pelmet.

fixed taffeta curtains

Although the taffeta curtains look rather grand, this treatment could also be used on a smaller scale. The system of stringing means that the tops of the curtains always remain fixed together, but by pulling up the string you can open and close the curtains.

1 Staple the looped side of the touch-and-close tape to the inside edge of the pelmet, about 1cm from the bottom edge. Attach the screw eyes to the underside of the board, in a straight row, about 10cm apart and with the middle two overlapping. Add an extra one just inside each back corner to take the cording. Fit the board about 5cm back from the inside front of the pelmet and fix to the wall. Screw a cleat to each side of the window frame.

2 The valance is made from a triple width of silk taffeta. To calculate the length required, add 4cm to the required depth, and match the pattern. Overlock the raw edges, then machine stitch the pieces of silk together, ensuring that the repeats match up (see p181). Press the seams open. To avoid snagging the delicate fabric, fit a new machine needle and use a Teflon foot if you have one. You could also stitch through a layer of tissue paper to protect the silk.

3 Pin, baste and machine the bias binding right sides together to the sides and bottom of the valance, making a small mitre at each corner. Turn the binding over to enclose the raw edge, mitre the corners and pin, baste and slip stitch (see p183) it to the back and press.

4 Thread a large-eyed needle with a long length of strong thread and sew a row of running stitch (see p183) 2cm down from the top of the valance. Work a second parallel row 1cm further down, ensuring that the stitches are in line. Knot the threads together at one side and pull them up from the other end until the valance is the same length as the hooked side of the touch-and-close tape. Knot the ends securely and trim, then arrange the gathers evenly.

5 Pin, baste and hand stitch the tape to the front of the valance, covering the running stitches. Attach the valance to the pelmet board.

6 One curtain is made from a width and a half of fabric. Work out the length you will need by adding 37.5cm plus any pattern repeats to the finished drop. Overlock the raw edges and with right sides together, pin, baste and machine the half width to the outside edge of the full width. Make a 2cm double hem along each side by pressing under a 4cm fold, opening it out and folding in the raw edge to meet the crease. Turn in again along the original crease, then pin, baste and slip stitch in place. Press.

7 Fold and sew a 15cm double hem along the bottom of the curtain in the same way, weighing it

down with hem tape, which should be secured at both ends, (see p181) and finishing with herringbone stitch (see p183).

8 Press in a 1.5cm turning along the top edge of the curtain, then press in a further 6cm. Pin, baste and machine the heading tape on top of this so that the turning is enclosed. Pull the tape up so that the curtain is the required width and secure with a knot (see p182). Ensure that the gathers are even. Insert the curtain hooks at 8cm intervals.

9 Lay the curtain out on a flat surface with right side facing downwards. Starting two-fifths of the drop from the top corner of the leading edge, sew the first cording ring 15cm in from the edge. Sew three more rings at regular intervals, running up at a 45-degree angle to the opposite edge, ending just beyond the half-width seam.

10 Tie one end of the cord securely to the first ring, securing with a few stitches, and thread the second end up through the other rings. Tie it loosely to the top ring so that it stays in place until you are ready to gather the folds.

11 Make the second curtain in the same way, checking that the pattern will match up across the pair and reversing the leading edge. Hang both curtains within the pelmet, threading the unstitched ends of the cords through the corner screw eyes. Pull the cords up on either side to gather the curtains into billowing folds and secure around the cleats.

materials & equipment

Silk taffeta

Touch-and-close tape, the width of the finished valance

Bias binding

75mm pencil pleat heading tape

Hem tape

Decorative pelmet

Length of 75 x 25mm board to fit pelmet

Screw eyes and curtain hooks

2 cleats with fixing screws

Screwdriver

8 cording rings and blind cord

Buttonhole or strong thread

Staple gun

Sewing kit

inverted pleat blind

On a huge window a plain, straight Roman blind would look heavy and too structured, so an alternative is required. Here, with the addition of some large, inverted pleats, which help to break the horizontal lines, a much softer treatment is achieved. Soft and tactile velvet ribbon outlines the blind.

inverted pleat blind

This is also called a London blind. It is made along the lines of a Roman blind but the inverted pleats give it a softer look. This blind measures 150cm wide by 220cm. The inverted pleats and the back are made from a plain fabric. The front and back are made up separately, then sewn together like a bag and turned inside out. The secret to this blind is to match up the pattern across the front panels.

I Cut the centre panel of patterned fabric (this one is 80cm wide). This should measure the drop of the blind plus 3cm, and the width plus 3cm. Press under a 1.5cm hem along both sides. Cut two side pieces, which when turned in 1.5cm at the sides, measure 35cm wide and will match the pattern of the centre panel. Cut to the same drop as the centre panel. For the pleats,

cut two pieces of the plain fabric the same drop as the other pieces, and about 42cm wide. Mark the centre of the top and bottom edges with a pin.

2 Place the centre panel right side up on a flat surface and with the side hems opened out. Lay one of the plain pieces, wrong side up, over the top and line it up with the right side. Pin and baste together 1.5cm from the edge and machine stitch.

3 Open out and lay right side up. Place the right-hand patterned side piece, wrong side up, along the right edge. Pin, baste and machine together 1.5cm from the edges. Join the second plain piece to the left side of the centre panel as in

step 2. Open out and place the left-hand patterned side piece, wrong side up, along the edge of the plain piece. Pin, baste and machine 1.5cm from the edges.

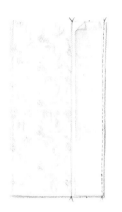

4 Press the four seams, with wrong sides facing, to give a crisp edge to the pleats.

5 Bring the two long edges of the centre and right-hand panels together and line them up with the two pin marks on the plain fabric. Fold the plain fabric out at either side to make an inverted pleat and press it into position. Repeat for the left-hand pleat. Pin together the top and bottom edges of the two pleats and baste. Machine 1cm from the edges, taking in all the layers.

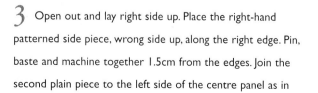

6 Cut a piece of plain fabric to the same size as the pleated blind. Place the blind on a flat surface right side up and lay the lining fabric over it wrong side up. Baste together on all four sides. Machine down leaving a 30cm gap in the centre of the bottom edge. Turn right sides out, close the gap with neat, tiny hand stitches and press.

7 Baste, then hand stitch the velvet ribbon to the two sides and bottom edge of the blind.

8 Sew four rows of five blind rings onto the back of the blind, in line with the centre of the pleats. Start by sewing four rings along the bottom edge. Measure 50cm up and sew four more, making sure to catch in both sides of the pleat on the middle two rings, as this will help keep the blind neatly folded. Sew on a further three rows, each 50cm apart.

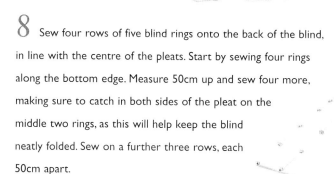

9 Cut a piece of touch-and-close tape the width of the blind. Separate the two pieces and hand stitch the looped side to the wrong side of the blind, 0.5cm down from the top edge.

10 Cover the batten with plain fabric and attach the hooked side of the touch-and-close tape to the front using a staple gun. Attach four screw eyes to the base in line with the rows of blind rings. To complete the blind, fix the batten in place and follow the instructions for stringing on p179.

---

materials
& equipment

Patterned fabric

Plain fabric for pleats and
lining the back

Velvet ribbon

Touch-and-close tape

Wooden batten, the width of the
blind

4 screw eyes

Blind rings

Blind cord

Cleat with fixing screws

Staple gun

Sewing kit

reversible curtain

A door which gives directly into a room from the outside benefits from a curtain
that uses two complementary fabrics and looks pretty from both sides. A single
reversible tie-back holds the curtain away when not needed.

reversible curtain

A versatile heading, the button-on tabs make hanging the curtain a snip, so the curtain can easily be reversed. Because the curtain butts right into the wall, special flat disc finials are used with the chunky wooden pole. A heavy cotton interlining separates the fabrics and provides extra draught insulation. The curtain is made from a single width of fabric, so ensure your chosen fabric has sufficient width.

I The linen, checked fabric and interlining should all be the same width: trim as necessary if they do not already match up. Cut one drop each of embroidered linen and checked fabric the drop required plus 13cm. Cut the interlining the drop required plus 3cm.

2 Place the checked fabric and the linen right sides together on a flat surface, so that the linen is uppermost. Lay the interlining over the top and align the top and side edges. Pin and baste the top and sides together, then machine stitch leaving a 3cm seam allowance. Clip the top corners.

3 Fold up and press a 1cm turning at the bottom edge, then turn up a further 9cm hem incorporating the interlining with the linen. Pin, baste and herringbone stitch (see p183) the linen and slip stitch (see p183) the checked fabric. Turn right side out and press.

4 Cover the buttons with checked fabric following the manufacturer's instructions. Mark seven points at regular intervals along the top of the curtain, 3.5cm from the edges and 3cm down from the top. Sew on two buttons at each point, one on each side of the curtain.

5 For each of the seven tabs, cut a 10cm x 36cm strip of checked fabric on the cross for the back and an 8cm x 34cm strip from a plain bit of the linen for the front. Press under and baste a 1.5cm turning on all four sides of a checked strip, mitring the corners. Press under 1.5cm on the two long sides of a linen strip, then on the short sides, without mitring. Baste down.

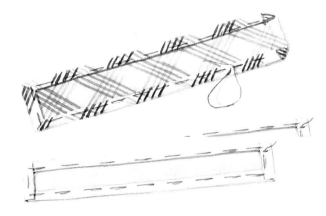

6 Place the front and back wrong sides together, centring the linen exactly. Pin, baste and machine stitch close to the edge of the linen. Repeat for the other six tabs. Make two buttonholes by hand or machine in the centre of each tab,

8cm apart, to fit over the covered buttons.

Slip the tabs over the buttons.

... the tie-back

7 To make the tie back, cut a checked strip measuring 22cm x 75cm across the grain of the fabric for the back. Position an 18cm x 71cm piece of buckram centrally on the wrong side and fold over the raw edges of the check, mitring the corners. Pin and baste down 1cm from the edges. Cut a strip of linen measuring 9cm x 72cm for the front. Fold in and press 1.5cm turnings as for the tabs, then with right side facing upwards, position the linen centrally over the buckram.

Pin the front and back together, starting from the centre and working outwards. Baste and machine through all the layers, close to the edge of the linen.

8 For the spaghetti ties, cut two narrow strips of the check fabric 5cm x 34cm. For each tie, fold the long sides together with right sides facing, then pin, baste and machine a 0.5cm seam down the long side and one short side. Turn the fabric inside out with a knitting needle, press flat and tie a knot 2cm from each end. Hand stitch the open end and sew centrally to the back of the tie back, 3cm in from the edges.

9 Hang the curtain at the window. Screw the hook into the wall and wrap the tie-back around it, securing the ties.

Country style is the complete antidote to stressful living. The modern country interior is full of comfort elements – old linen, rubbed paint, fresh field flowers, and quirky rooms. It is a style as comfortable in town as out, and has about it an easy and relaxed feel. This chapter explores window treatments that are a little out of the ordinary, such as a curtain made of ribbons and beads, to inspire you to look around you and use what you may have at home. Thus an old worn quilt is revived to frame a view, timeless cotton gingham makes a lovely pair of curtains with a shaped valance, and red gingham ribbon outlines crisp white organdie. An antique monogrammed linen sheet is transformed into curtains, and fresh green and white roll-up blinds transform a laundry. Don't be afraid to use colour and pattern, but do use them to complement a room, not just for the sake of it.

country

The window treatments illustrated on these pages embody the country style. The projects, which begin overleaf, offer various interpretations of the look for the modern home.

sequined blind

It would be sad to hide a lovely tall window with a handsome architrave behind curtains. Instead, an unlined blind with small, loose pleats sits perfectly in the inner reveal. This woven cotton fabric looks as fresh from the outside as from within, and a little sparkle and glamour has been added in the form of a sequined edging.

sequined blind

An unlined pleated blind can work well on its own as a minimal window covering and also in conjunction with curtains. If you use a woven fabric, such as this one, it looks wonderful from outside the window too. A crisp linen or cotton lends itself well to this type of blind, as the pleats are ironed in and will successfully keep their shape. The pleats are very small and look more tailored this way. This treatment is not well suited to a very wide window, as the pleats begin to collapse. Try a Roman blind with wooden dowels instead.

I   Press the linen and cut a piece the size of the blind required plus 5cm in drop and 4cm in width for hem allowances. Add an extra 0.5cm per pleat and a little extra for the bottom pleat to the length. Lay the linen, wrong side up, on a flat surface. Turn in and press a 2cm hem along each side, open out and press in half. Refold to form a double 1cm hem. Pin, baste and machine stitch. Make a 3cm hem along the bottom edge in the same way but don't machine the sides as this forms the pocket for the dowel.

2   To mark the position of the first pleat, measure up 24cm from each bottom corner and mark with a pin at both side edges. Work out the

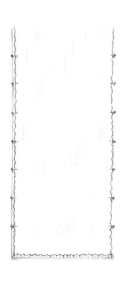

position of the other pleats by dividing the rest of the blind evenly into sections of about 20cm. Mark off each pleat with a pin at both side edges, again taking the measurement from each bottom corner to ensure the lines are straight.

3   Fold the first pleat under to the right side of the blind. Press firmly along the fold using spray starch to ensure a sharp crease, then machine the pleat 0.5cm from the edge.

4   Turn the blind over and, with right side facing, press in a starched fold at the first 20cm mark. Turn the blind back to the wrong side, then fold and machine the next pleat as in step 3. Continue pressing in folds as you work your way

up the blind, making sure they are accurate and straight.

5   Sew two blind rings onto the back of the first sewn pleat about 12–14cm in from the edges. Continue sewing rings onto the back of each pleat, making sure they all line up.

6 Insert the dowel into the open bottom hem and hand stitch the openings to secure. Sew a length of sequined tape along the bottom of the blind. Drill two holes through the front of the batten for fixing. Cover the batten with linen using the staple gun, and pierce the fabric over the holes with a bradawl. Insert the two screw eyes on the bottom edge, the same distance from the ends as the blind rings. Check the length of the blind against the window and trim away any extra fabric. Staple the top of the blind to the batten, overlapping the raw edge to the back.

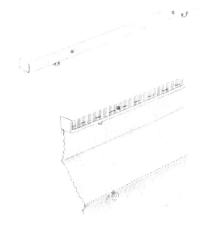

Follow the instructions for stringing the blind on p179.

Follow the instructions for stringing the blind on p179.

materials & equipment

Linen

Sequined tape

Thin wooden dowel, the width of the blind

Wooden batten, the width of the blind, and 2 screw eyes

Blind rings and cord

Cleat with fixing screws

Spray starch

Staple gun

Drill and bradawl

Sewing kit

scalloped curtains

For deep, recessed windows, portière rods work a treat, as they can be opened right
back to reveal maximum light or closed for privacy, or partially opened for a
combination of the two. A crisp red and white cotton stripe is backed with a pretty
floral and sewn with small scallops on two sides.

scalloped curtains

Portière rods have so many uses, especially for attic or inward opening windows and doors which need to be treated individually. They are easy to install, require the minimum fullness, and swing away into reveals when not needed.

A gathered top is made by bunching the fabric tightly on a pocket heading. There is a small stand-up above the portière rod, adding a bit of crispness to the look. The scallops are a bit painstaking to make, particularly when lining up the stripe, but worth it for the end effect. Making a card template for them is essential, and using two materials of the same weight is also helpful for when it comes to washing them!

1   For one curtain, cut a piece of the floral fabric and a piece of striped fabric to the size required, adding 3cm for turnings to the total drop and 3cm to the width.

2   To work out the size of the scallops, divide the total drop by the number you require. Make a circular card template using this measurement for the diameter, then draw a line across the centre. (A drop of 120cm requires 20 scallops, each 6cm wide.)

3   Lay the two pieces of fabric right sides together on a flat surface. Starting 2cm from the top corner, use tailor's chalk and a long ruler to mark a line a radius width plus 1cm in from the edge down the fabric, then do the same along the bottom edge. Matching the diameter line on the template with the chalk line, draw a series of semi-circles along the side and bottom edges. Pin, baste and machine these two sides together, allowing 1cm for turnings, then join the unmarked side with a 2cm seam.

4   Cut away the excess fabric around the scallops, clipping between them and into the curves so that they will lie flat. Turn right sides out. For a perfect finish, tease out the curved edge of each scallop between finger and thumb, basting with small stitches as you go before pressing. Press under a 1cm turning around the top edge of the curtain, then pin, baste and machine down.

5   To make the rod pocket, cut a strip of floral fabric the width of the curtain plus 2cm by the circumference of the rod, plus a 1cm seam allowance. Press under a 1cm turning at each end and machine down, then press a 0.5cm turning along each long edge.

6   Mark a chalk line on the back of the curtain, 2cm down from the top. With right side upwards, pin and baste the top edge of the pocket along the line, then pin and

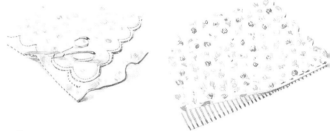

baste the lower edge to the curtain. Machine both edges, close
to the fold. Slide the rod into the rod pocket with the scalloped
edge facing outwards and the top is arranged in neat gathers.

Make the second curtain in the same way, but with the scallops
on the opposite side.

materials & equipment

Floral fabric

Striped fabric

2 portière rods

Card for template

Pair of compasses

Long ruler

Sewing kit

quilt curtain

For a quick and effective window treatment, an all-in-one
curtain and valance can be created to frame a view or just add
softness to a window. An old quilt has been adapted, simply
outlined in ricrac braid and gathered on an expansion pole.

quilt curtain

Because of the thickness of the quilt, you need no lining for this curtain. A small pocket is sewn to the back to receive an expansion rod or tension wire. Worn blankets make a good alternative to a quilt.

I   Measure the window, and with tailor's chalk and a ruler mark out the shape of your curtain so that the two sides are the same width and the depth of the 'valance' looks in correct proportion to the side panels. You will need to cut away a large enough area from the centre to allow sufficient light to come through without losing the impact of the fabric. You may prefer to work out the shape first by cutting out a toile from a sheet of calico pinned up at the window.

2   Cut out the central area and overlock all the raw edges. Place the curtain right side down and pin, baste and machine stitch 1cm hems on all the edges that require finishing, snipping into each of the inside corners and clipping the outside corners to allow for the thickness of the wadding.

3   Working on the wrong side of the curtain, pin, baste and machine the ricrac braid along the top, bottom and inside edges so that the curves peep out on the right side.

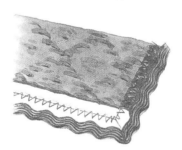

4   To make a pocket for the expansion rod, cut a strip of plain fabric the circumference of the rod plus 2cm by the width of the curtain panel plus 2cm for turnings. Press a 0.5cm turning along each long side, then press under and machine 1cm seams at either end. Pin, baste and machine the pocket 3cm down from the top of the curtain. If the curtain is to be hung from a tension wire the pocket can be narrower.

simple swag

In a north-facing bathroom a soft silk swag adds a degree of
sophistication and elegance. It also camouflages the
mechanism of a roller blind behind it that is needed for
privacy. The miniature red bobble fringe helps to delineate
the curve of the swag and adds a punch of colour.

simple swag

This very simple swag is made from a single straight length of fabric, which is used on its side to avoid joins. To form a relaxed shape, it is best to use a soft, malleable fabric such as rough silk. The tails of the swag hang down half the distance of the middle depth, which creates a wonderful curve.

1 Cut a length of fabric the width of the architrave plus the two swag lengths required. Press under a 1cm turning twice at both ends of the silk panel to make a double hem. Baste and machine stitch down. Silk has a tightly woven selvedge which doesn't usually fray and won't need hemming, but if your fabric frays at all at the sides or looks unfinished, neaten it with a very narrow hem.

2 Pin the bobble fringe to the right side of the fabric, along one long side. Align the selvedge of the bobble fringe with the edge of the fabric, so that the bobbles hang free of the fabric. Baste and machine down.

3 To make the ties, cut two strips of silk 10cm wide by 50cm long. Fold one in half lengthways, right sides facing. Baste and machine together along the long side and one short end, 1cm from the edge. Turn inside out using the end of a wooden spoon. Hand close the open end and press. Make the second tie in the same way.

4 Fix the swag directly onto the top of the window frame. Fold the plain edge of the fabric in half and mark with a pin. Staple this point to the centre top of the frame and continue stapling out to each corner. Gather the loose fabric up into folds at one end, making a series of neat pleats at the side. Tie up securely with a length of string. Fold the other side in the same way.

5 Wrap the ties around the gathered ends over the string, and knot at the top. Turn the knot to the back of the swag. Hammer in a small nail to hold each tie in place and prevent them slipping down.

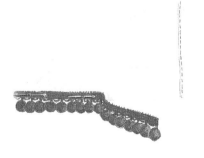

materials
& equipment

Length of rough silk, twice the

width of the window frame

plus extra for ties

Bobble fringe, the same length as

the silk

String

Staple gun

Hammer and 2 small nails

Wooden spoon

Sewing kit

pencil pleat floral curtains

A vibrantly pretty floral-printed cotton is used for a
traditional pair of curtains. The edges are outlined in a
contrasting red binding which adds some definition, and the
headings are made using a pencil pleat curtain tape.

pencil pleat floral curtains

These curtains have been made with two widths in each curtain. The heading tape has been sewn on deliberately low so that the top of the curtains fall slightly forward from the pole. A layer of buckram has also been added to the top of the curtains to give extra body and crispness to the heading.

1 Cut two drops of the floral fabric, the length required plus 3cm, taking into account before cutting any pattern repeat when joining the drops (see p179). Lay them, right sides facing, on a flat surface. Pin, baste and machine stitch together 1.5cm from one side edge. Make regular snips into the selvedges, to release any tension, then open out the seam and press. With the curtain wrong side up, pin and baste the length of buckram in place, aligning it with the top and side edges.

2 Cut two drops of lining, the length required plus 3cm. Join together as in step 1. Lay the lining over the curtain edge to edge with the right sides facing each other. Pin, baste, then machine together along both sides, top (catching in the buckram) and bottom, leaving a 20cm opening in the centre of the bottom

edge. Trim the corner triangles, turn right side out and press. Close the opening by hand with slip stitch (see p183).

3 To make the binding, cut 10cm wide bias strips from the contrast fabric. Using tailor's chalk and a long ruler, mark a line at 45 degrees to the selvedge, from one bottom corner up to the opposite side. Rule a series of parallel lines, 10cm apart, then cut along the chalk marks. Cut enough strips to join up and surround the curtain on all four sides. Sew the strips together to form a continuous length of binding. Lay the first two strips right sides facing and at right angles to each other. Baste and machine, leaving a 0.75cm seam allowance. Open out and press the seam.

Trim the corners so they lie flat with the edges. Repeat to form the length required.

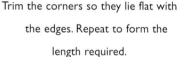

4 With right sides together and edges lined up, pin the bias strip along one side of the curtain, starting at a bottom outside corner. Baste together 2.5cm from the edge. When you reach the top edge, pin up to 1.5cm from the corner, then pinch the binding into a fold. Continue pinning and basting along the top edge and repeat the pinch for the next two corners, until you arrive back at the starting point. Overlap the binding by 1.5cm. Machine along the basting line. Stitch all the way to the corner folds, then stop, and continue stitching on the other side. Turn the curtain over and bring the binding over, folding it under 2.5cm, pinning as you go, folding the corners in as neatly as possible. Then baste the binding all round the curtain. Slip stitch the binding to the curtain. At the corner where the two ends of the binding meet, hand stitch to form a neat corner mitre.

5 Cut a length of heading tape about 6cm wider than the curtain. Pin it to the wrong side, about 5cm from the top edge leaving an equal amount of tape overlapping each side. To attach it to the top of the curtain, follow the instructions for attaching heading tape on p182.

Make the second curtain in the same way. Hang the curtains.

materials
& equipment
Floral fabric
Plain fabric for contrast edging
Lining fabric
Pencil pleat heading tape, 9cm wide
Buckram, 14cm wide, the width
of the ungathered curtains
Long ruler
Sewing kit

In a light-filled laundry occasional protection from the sun and privacy are both needed: the solution is a series of little roll-up blinds made from the finest striped cotton. You can control each window independently with a simple cord and cleat mechanism. The blinds have metal eyelets so the cord can glide easily, and each blind is attached to a wooden batten with touch-and-close tape.

roll-up blinds

roll-up blinds

These blinds really are easy to make and look so fresh and simple. The key is to cut the fabric straight so the stripes don't veer off. The top hems are folded over to give three layers as the cotton is very thin – it is easier to insert metal eyelets into thicker layers of fabric. I used woven cotton, which is completely reversible, and rolled the fabric forward. The instructions for the stringing are for forward rolls. If you want the rolls to go to the back because the fabric is printed, change the stringing to suit.

1 Cut a length of fabric the drop required plus 25cm and 5cm wider than the finished blind. Lay the fabric wrong side up. Press in a 0.5cm turning along each side, then press in another 2cm. Baste and machine stitch down.

2 Make a double hem along the top by pressing down 10cm, then a further 10cm. Baste and machine down.

3 Mark two pairs of points 10cm apart along the top of the blind, 5cm down from the edge and about 15cm from the outside edges. Fix an eyelet to each point using an eyelet maker and making sure that the right sides are on the front of the blind.

4 Pin the looped side of the touch-and-close tape on the reverse of the blind at the top and slip stitch down (see p183).

5 Staple the bottom raw edge of the blind to the dowel rod.

6 Drill holes in the underside of the batten 15cm in from each end for the screw eyes, and another two holes in line with these through the front of the batten for fixing. Cover the batten with fabric using a staple gun. Pierce the fabric over the holes with a bradawl and attach the screw eyes. Staple the hooked piece of touch-and-close tape to the front of the batten and pierce the holes with a bradawl. Attach the batten to the window using long screws.

7 Attach the blind with the touch-and-close tape. Following the diagram, string the blind so it rolls forward. Adjust the cords so the blind rolls up evenly. Knot the ends together and fix the cleat.

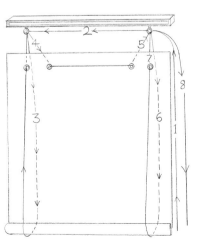

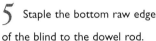

materials & equipment

Woven cotton

Touch-and-close tape, the width of the blind

Waxed string, blind cord or rolled cording

Thin wooden dowel, the width of the blind

Wooden batten, the width of the blind

Cleat with fixing screws

Eyelet kit

Screw eye

Long sjcrews

Staple gun

Bradawl

Screwdriver

Drill

Sewing kit

ribbon curtain

This is as close to no-sew curtains as it gets! Ribbons are attached to the pole with hand-sewn loops, and the beads are attached using strong embroidery cotton. This is one project on which your imagination can roam freely. The Perspex pole adds a little sparkle and is held in place with shower curtain pole ends.

1 Calculate the circumference of the pole by wrapping the end of one ribbon around it, overlapping by a 1cm seam allowance and measuring this length.

2 Mark a seam at the point on both sides of the ribbon where it will just slide on and off easily.

3 Using this measurement and with right side to wrong side, baste and stab stitch a seam for the channel at the top end of each ribbon.

4 Arrange the beads in varying quantities and assortments. For each ribbon, double thread a needle with the embroidery cotton and make a firm knot big enough to keep the beads on. Thread the beads and finish with a similarly firm knot. Turn up the ends of the ribbons twice and hold in place by stitching the beads on.

5 Cut a pole to the width required, allowing for the fittings. Put the fittings on and, with a pencil, mark the position of the screws in the window. Use a bradawl to make a hole on each of the pencil marks.

6 Feed the ribbons on to the pole. Support the pole while putting the first two screws in, one either side. Put in the other screws and tighten in rotation.

materials
& equipment

*Various ribbons of differing
lengths and widths*

Beads

Perspex pole

Shower rail fittings and screws

Screwdriver and screws

Bradawl

Cotton embroidery thread

Sewing Kit

pleated organdie curtains

In a girl's bedroom pleated white organdie curtains are reminiscent of gymslips. Fresh red-and-white gingham ribbon is used for binding the edges, holding down the pleats, and for the ties. With only the curtains, the room can be flooded with light, yet remain private. A fitted blackout roller blind behind the curtains keeps out unwanted light.

pleated organdie curtains

Cotton organdie has such a wonderful crispy billowiness about it that it always looks fresh. It also launders beautifully. These curtains have tightly pleated headings that are held in place with two layers of ribbon, gingham over picot. The side hems are wrapped with the same gingham ribbon used as a binding. The tighter the pleats the more the bottom will balloon.

I   Cut one and a half drops of organdie plus 18cm. The fabric won't be lined so the drops need to be joined very neatly with no exposed raw edges. A flat fell seam gives a smooth and flat finish. Pin and baste the two pieces together with right sides facing. Machine stitch 1.5cm from the edge, then press both turnings to one side. Trim the lower turning to 0.75cm.

Press under a narrow hem along the edge of the upper turning, then fold down over the lower turning to enclose all the raw edges. Slip stitch (see p183) to the wrong side of the curtain.

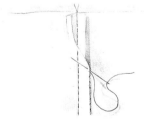

2   Make a double hem along each side. Press in 2cm, open out and fold in a 1cm crease so the raw edge lines up exactly with the first crease. Press again.

3   Turn down a 2cm hem at the top of the curtain and press.

4   Working from the leading edge out, fold the top 25cm of the curtain into a regular series of pleats, each approximately 2.5cm wide. Pin them at the top and bottom as you work. Press the pleats only, then baste at the top and bottom.

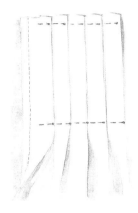

5   Cut two pieces each of the gingham ribbon and the picot braid, each the width of the curtain plus 1cm. Place a strip of picot braid along the top edge of the curtain and centre a piece of ribbon over it, leaving 0.5cm overlap at either end. Pin and baste. Machine down with two rows of stitching, along the top and bottom edges of the ribbon. Trim off the excess. Sew the other length of braid and ribbon along the bottom edge of the pleats in the same way.

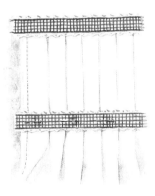

6   Finish the bottom edge with a double hem. Fold up and press a 14cm turning, then open out. Fold up 7cm and press, then herringbone stitch down (see p183).

7   Cut two lengths of gingham ribbon the drop of the curtain plus 1cm. Fold down the two short ends 0.5cm each and machine down. Fold the ribbon in half lengthways and press. Wrap over the side edge of the curtain, enclosing the hem. Pin, baste and machine down.

8   Cut six lengths of wider gingham ribbon 40cm each (or enough to space about 30cm apart). Fold in half and hand sew to the wrong side of the top edge.

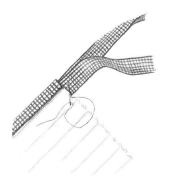

Make the second curtain in the same way.

materials & equipment

Cotton organdie
Gingham ribbon, 2.5cm wide for the ties and 1.75cm wide for being laid on picot edging
Picot braid, slightly wider than the gingham
Sewing kit

antique linen curtain

materials
& equipment
Antique monogrammed sheet

Satin ribbon for ties

Thin brass pole with brackets and

brass rings

Small split curtain rings

Sewing kit

This is such an easy and simple curtain treatment, and especially useful when you want to cover only the lower half of a window. It still permits full light from the top and diffused light through the linen. Because monogrammed sheets are made for the top to turn back on a bed and reveal the embroidery, they are ideally suited to curtains with a self-valance. In fact, on this one I only cut some of the drop away at the bottom and was able to use the existing side hems. If you need to narrow down a sheet to fit a window, cut away equal amounts from both sides and make a small double hem, preferably hand stitched. For the amount of drop on the valance, fold over the top edge and hold the sheet up to your window: for a half window it should measure between a quarter and a third of the drop, whereas with a full-length curtain it should be nearer a fifth of the drop.

I   Turn over the top edge of the sheet to the valance drop required (see above) and press in place. Pin and baste along the fold. Measure the width and divide it by eight, then mark off each section with a pin.

2   Fold and pin a very small box pleat at each mark and at either end. Press in place and hand stitch from the back to hold the pleats in place.

3   Sew a split curtain ring to the back of each pleat and attach each one to a brass ring.

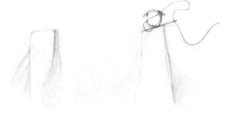

4   To conceal the split ring, wind a length of satin ribbon through both rings several times and tie the ends into a neat bow.

Timeless, fresh, and classically French, purple gingham is used liberally both for dressing the bed and the window. A slightly shaped, gathered valance fixed to a wooden board hides the tracks of the curtains. The curtains are interlined and lined with a matching purple cotton chambray, and held back using wooden bosses covered in chambray and grosgrain ribbon. Velvet violets add a finishing touch.

gingham curtains

gingham curtains

Wooden pelmet boards have been used for centuries to hold pelmets, valances and the fixings for curtains. They can hide many faults, and are very useful when proportions need disguising. In this case, the window is somewhat low in the room, so I took the pelmet board up higher over the window to give the illusion of more height. Always make sure that the bottom of the valance covers the top of the window or it will look unsightly. Instead of using heading tape to gather the gingham valance, I made a little pocket and threaded through piping cord and pulled it up. It makes it look slightly less 'perfect', to suit the room. A little pale-mauve trimming was used to outline the curved edge of the valance. Because gingham is usually very thin, I used an interlining as well as a lining, which helps give shape to the curtains.

... the valance

I Cut three drops of the gingham, the length required plus 23cm. With right sides facing, join the three widths by pinning, basting and machine stitching them together along the selvedges. Clip into the selvedges at 10cm intervals to release the tension and press the seams flat. Repeat for the domette and the chambray lining.

2 Fold the gingham in half width ways and place on a flat surface. Lay a length of hem tape along the bottom so that it forms a gentle curve between a point 22cm in from the two corners to a point 10cm along the fold. Draw a chalk line following this curve and pin the two sides together, 1cm away from the line. Cut along the curve. Use the gingham as a template and cut the chambray and domette to the same shape.

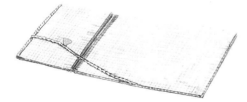

3 Open out the gingham with right side facing upwards. Place the chambray over it with right side down, then lay the domette on top, aligning all the edges. Press, pin, baste and machine a 1.5cm seam along both sides and the curve, leaving a 1cm gap in the seams. Snip into the curve and clip the corners. Turn right sides out and press.

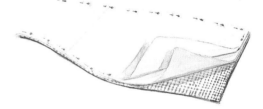

4 Press under a 5cm turning around the top of the valance. Pin the front and back together and slip stitch (see p183). Using the straight line across the gingham as a guide, pin, baste and machine a line 3.5cm from the top. Sew a second line 1.5cm below to make a channel. Cut a length of piping cord slightly longer than the finished width of the valance. Fix a safety pin to one end and secure the other end to the gap in the side seam. Feed the pin through the channel and gather the fabric to the length and two sides of the pelmet board.

Stitch down the other end of the cord, cutting off any surplus. Arrange the gathers into neat, even folds.

5 Separate the two parts of the touch-and-close tape. Pin the looped side to the back of the valance so that it covers the channel and slip stitch down. Sew the pink floral braid along the bottom of the valance. Staple the remaining length of touch-and-close tape to the top edge of the pelmet board.

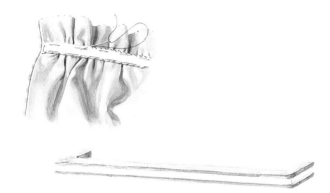

materials & equipment

for the valance and curtains

Gingham

Domette interlining

Chambray lining

Pink floral braid

Plain piping cord

Touch-and-close tape, to fit around the pelmet board

Hem tape

Pelmet board with a 20cm return

2 angle brackets

Heading tape

Track and pulleys

Staple gun

Sewing kit and safety pin

... the curtains

6 Each curtain is made from a single width of gingham. To calculate the length, measure the total drop and add 5cm for the heading and 10cm for the hem. Lay the chambray and gingham right sides together with the gingham face down. Cut the interlining so that it is 10cm shorter than the other fabrics and lay it over the chambray, aligning the top edges. Pin, baste and machine the sides and top, leaving a 1.5cm seam allowance. Clip the corners.

7 For the open hem, fold and press a 1cm turning around the bottom edge of the gingham and chambray, then turn up and press a further 9cm. Pin, baste and slip stitch the gingham hem and herringbone stitch (see p183) the chambray to the interlining. Turn the curtain right sides out and press. Add the heading tape (see p182). Repeat for the second curtain.

... the bosses

8 For each boss, cut a 10cm wide circle of MDF with a jigsaw and sand off any rough edges. Cut a 10cm length of dowelling. Drill holes for the screws in the centre of one side of the circle and both ends of the dowelling.

9 Cut two circles of chambray and a circle of bump, 0.75cm wider all round than the MDF. Glue one piece of chambray to the MDF, positioning it centrally over the side with the screw hole. When the glue is dry, pierce through the fabric and into the hole with a bradawl. Fold the surplus fabric over the sides, and stick down, snipping out the excess as necessary to give a smooth finish. Glue the bump to the other side of the circle and cover with the second piece of chambray, sticking the sides down as before.

10 Glue the flat side of the velvet piping cord around the side of the boss so that the cord is just proud of the bump-covered face. Cover it with the grosgrain and floral braids, beginning and ending in roughly the same position and taking care not to overlap.

11 Cut a length of chambray to cover the dowelling and overlap the end. Glue it in place and use a craft knife to trim away the excess for a neat finish.

12 Screw the boss to the dowelling and finish off by gluing a velvet flower to the centre front. Repeat for the second boss.

Hang the curtains on a track with a pulley and mount the valance above the window. Fix the bosses to the wall.

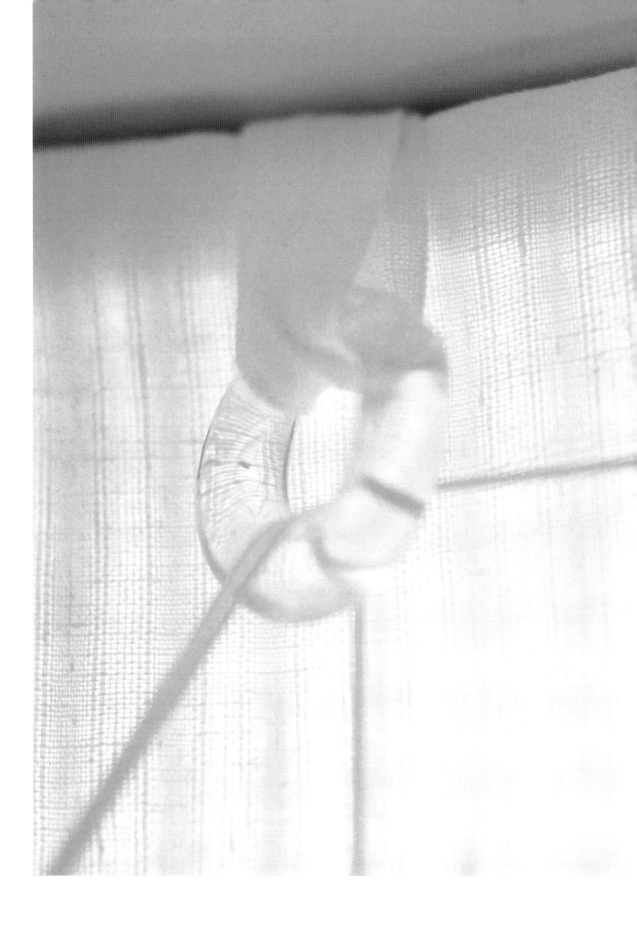

part 3
essentials

Curtain making is a logical business, and, rather like mathematics, it relies on a few basic rules on which you build up an inventory of techniques. This section of the book sets out these basics, from measuring and cutting fabrics to mastering specific stitches. Accuracy in curtain making is paramount. Working out quantities, drops, widths and repeats are the basics that will make your window treatments work and look professional.

decorative hangings

Exposed curtain poles are one of the most popular methods for hanging curtains. Poles are held up with brackets and are easily fixed to a wall. Curtains can be attached to poles in many ways. Fabric ties or tabs can be attached directly, or curtains can be attached to rings which slide onto the pole. Most rings have little metal eyelets at the bottom to take curtain hooks and heading tape. Some rings have powerful clips on them that grip the fabric and make a very useful 'no sew' heading. Otherwise, curtains can be slotted directly onto poles with pocket headings.

Traditionally, poles and rings were made from wood or brass, but now they come in anything from translucent Perspex to thin wrought iron. Wooden poles come in a variety of thicknesses and can be stained or painted. Metal poles also come in many widths and finishes and can even be made to bend around a bay window. Most poles are available fitted with cording tracks for easy opening and closing. Many poles come in kit form from department stores and can be cut down to fit. This makes the whole process less expensive and, with careful measuring and planning, an easy option.

hanging

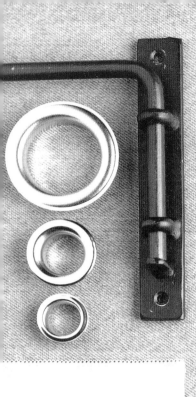

practicalities

Most curtains are made using a slotted heading tape which is sewn to the top of the curtain. There are many different kinds of heading tape available, depending on your need, but broadly speaking they range from narrow tape for lightweight curtains, to translucent tape for sheers, to tapes that can be pulled up to form triple pleats. Plastic or metal hooks slot into the pockets and then are fixed to a glider on a track. The tape gathers up with string that is threaded through it, so that the fabric can be gathered evenly. When heading tape is not used, the curtains are finished with a handmade heading and there are special hooks to attach to the track. Tracks come in a huge variety and perform many functions. The best way to learn about them is either to go to a specialist shop that displays different kinds so you can decide what best suits your requirements, or to look through catalogues.

Other methods of hanging curtains include metal eyelets and tension wire. The eyelets are inserted into the heading of the curtains using a special eyelet tool. A metal cable is threaded through and held taught with brackets. Metal portière rods are fixed to the side of the wall via brackets in which metal arms are slotted which can rotate 180 degrees. The curtains have a pocket heading which is slotted over the metal arms. Spring-loaded expansion rods are useful for recessed windows, as they can be slotted into the opening using no fixings. They will not support heavy curtains, but are excellent for hanging panels and sheers.

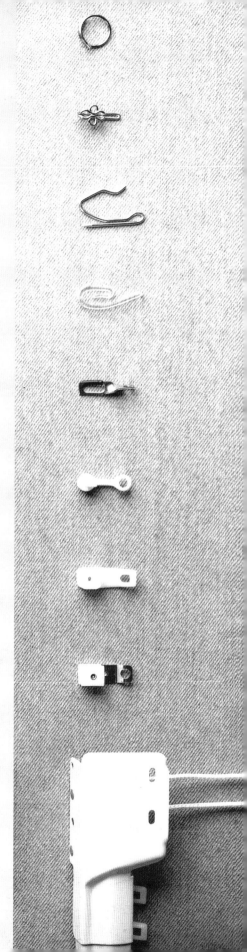

basic techniques

All the basics are grouped in one easy-to-use, illustrated reference section. Readers should familiarise themselves with these techniques before embarking on any project. At the end of the section is a cross reference directory which tells you which projects to consult to find instructions on more detailed techniques, such as mitring a corner or making a French seam.

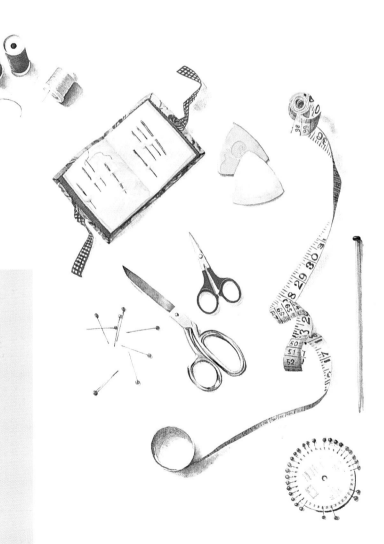

basic sewing kit

Sewing machine

Dressmaker's scissors

Embroidery scissors

Paper scissors

Tape measure

Tailor's chalk

Dressmaker's pins

Sewing needles

Basting cotton

MEASURING

preparation

Once you have chosen the type of window covering you are going to make and decided on the fabric and type of fittings, the next stage is to measure for and fix the fittings. It is always better to install any fittings before working out fabric quantities, as you will be able to take the most accurate measurements.

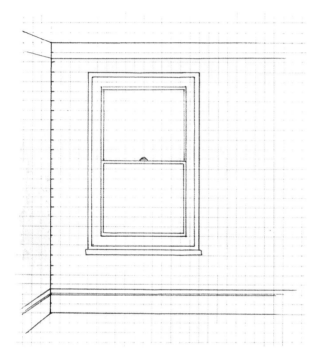

The first thing to do is to make a scaled sketch of the window. On a piece of squared paper draw an 'elevation' of your window wall. Allow one square per 10cm as a rough guide to scale. Draw the line of the floor, then measure up to the sill and draw in the window including any architraves. Add the line of the ceiling, including the depth of any mouldings. If the window is near a corner, measure the distance from the window to the corner and draw this in, as it will determine how the proportion of a fitting will look. Once you have this plan you can sketch in the fittings and see how they will look to scale (see diagram, above).

tracks and poles

Ideally, these should both be positioned about 10–15cm above the window and protrude about the same amount either side of the window. There are some important things to think about at this stage.

1 The bigger the window the bigger these distances should be.

2 Larger windows should have larger poles and brackets; proportion is everything.

3 Awkward proportions in a window or its positioning can be compensated for. Windows that are too narrow should have wider tracks or poles. Windows that are too low should have the fittings raised higher.

4 Poles and tracks should never be positioned at the same height or lower than the top of the window as this makes an unsightly line of light when the curtains are up. It is a mistake commonly made and quite unnecessary.

5 Where possible, brackets look best fixed to the wall not the architrave.

6 One of the commonest problems with ready-made fittings is that brackets are often not deep enough, and curtains brush against the window. This is to be avoided both aesthetically and practically. Air needs to circulate or condensation will form, and fabric should hang at least 6–8cm away from the window to look good. To compensate for this, either buy deeper brackets or

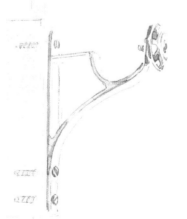

mount them on small wooden blocks (see diagram, left) which can be painted or papered to match the wall.

7 Install poles or tracks according to the manufacturer's instructions.

pelmet boards

Pelmet boards can hide tracks and alter proportions of windows most effectively. They should be made from a sturdy wood, such as plywood or pine, about 2.5cm thick. The depth of a pelmet board is usually about one-eighth of the drop of the curtain, but never less than 10cm, even for a small window. The width should be the same as for tracks or poles: about 10–15cm wider than the window plus 1.5cm extra on either side to allow for the thickness of the curtain fabric. It should be positioned 15–20cm above the window (unless you need to compensate for any shortcomings in the proportions as in point 3, p177). Pelmet boards are held in place with metal angle brackets (see diagram, below) and screwed to the wall above the window. Boards should either be covered in the same fabric as the curtains or painted a colour to match. Valances are attached most commonly with touch-and-close tape. Glue and staple the hooked side of the tape to the short sides and front edge of the board.

Tracks made specially for pelmet boards can be bought. Attach these according to the manufacturer's instructions, but remember that the track should be 1.5cm shorter than the board on both sides, to allow for the thickness of the curtains.

For fixed curtains, you should attach metal screw eyes to the underneath side of the board.

how to measure for curtain fabric

Always use a long retractable steel measuring tape. Decide which type of heading tape you will be using to determine the drop measurement. There are two main measurements that you need to work out fabric quantity: the length of the pole, track, or

pelmet board (see A on diagram, below) and the drop from these to the floor, or wherever you want your curtains to hang to (see B on diagram, below). The width (A) will determine the fullness or drops of fabric required.

Generally speaking, you should allow for one width to be between one-and-a-half and two times the length of the track, i.e. three or four cuts of fabric per pair. For a smaller window (where a track measures about 120cm) allow one width in each curtain. Note that lighter weight fabrics need more fullness and sheers need at least three widths in each curtain.

For the drop or length, you should measure as follows. For curtains hung from a pole, measure from the base of a curtain ring to the floor. For curtains hung from an exposed track, measure from the top of the heading tape to the floor (to make this easier you can hook a piece of heading tape to the track and measure). For curtains hung from a pelmet board, measure from the underside of the board to the floor. For curtains with eyelet

headings, measure from the top of the pole to the floor and add at least 4cm allowance above the eyelets.

Add in the hem and heading measurements (these are specified in each project). If you want the curtains to drape onto the floor or you are using tie-backs or Italian stringing, add 5–20cm to each drop.

If the fabric is patterned, you must add in the depth of the pattern repeat to each drop.

To recap, the formula for fabric quantity is: hook drop + hem + heading + pattern repeat, multiplied by the number of drops. Round this figure up to the nearest half metre. Check all measurements twice before ordering fabric.

Always check you have allowed enough fabric for valances, tie-backs or ties as well.

For lining and interlining, choose these the same width as the main fabric so that you can line up the seams. You will need about the same amount of fabric but without allowances for pattern repeats and without double hems.

how to measure for blind fabric

As with curtains, it is best to make and install the wooden batten before making the blind. Blinds can either be fitted into the recess of a window or they can be face fixed (i.e. over the top of the window). If you need to disguise the shape of a window, face fixing is best. Face fixing also takes away less natural light than a recess fitted blind.

For a recessed Roman blind, measure from the top of the wooden batten to the sill, and the width of the recess (see D and E on diagram, opposite) less 1cm either side. For a face-fixed

Roman blind, measure from the top of the wooden batten to about 5cm below the sill. Remember these are your finished blind measurements only.

fixing blinds

A face-fixed blind needs a wooden batten the width of the window plus 10–15cm either side, and should be fixed that same distance from the top of the window (see C on diagram, opposite). It should either be screwed directly into the wall or used with a small pair of brackets. The batten should be made from a piece of sturdy timber such as pine or plywood. It looks best covered with the same fabric as the blind or painted a matching colour. (If the batten is covered with fabric, use a bradawl to make holes in the fabric when installing to avoid the fabric twisting with the screws.) It will need the hooked side of the touch-and-close tape fixed to the long narrow edge with a staple gun (see diagram, above).

A recessed blind is also fixed using a wooden batten. This should measure 1cm less than the window reveal for easy fitting and can be screwed into the top or back of the recess. Other than that, it is made the same way as a face-fixed batten. For Roman blinds, you will need to attach screw eyes to the board for the cords, but it is best to put these in once the blind has been made and you can match the spaces exactly to the blind rings.

stringing a Roman blind

Make certain that you have sewn blind rings onto the back of the pleats as instructed in the relevant projects. Attach metal screw eyes to the bottom of the batten to line up with the rows of blind rings, then fix the batten to the wall or frame. For each vertical row of blind rings, cut a length of blind cord at least three times the drop of the blind. Decide which side of the window the blind is going to be fixed and attach the cleat. Working on the back of the blind and starting with the vertical row that is the farthest from the cleat side, knot the blind cord to the bottom ring, using a double knot. String the cord through each successive ring to the top. Repeat for all vertical rows of rings. Carefully attach the blind to the batten with the touch-and-close tape, ensuring that the cords stay in place. Run the

blind cords through the screw eyes so that they meet on the cleat side. (see diagram, above.) You need to keep the blind down and work in the confines of the back of it and the window. Keep the blind down, make sure it is straight, then gather the cords and pull up the pleats to ensure they look straight. Knot off the cord but make sure you leave a long enough length for when the blind is down. Check it carefully a few times. Attach the cord to a cord tidy or blind acorn, and cut off any excess cord.

For roller blinds, follow the manufacturer's instructions. For all other blinds, see the project instructions.

cutting the fabric

You need a large, flat, clean surface. A good sharp pair of dressmaker's scissors are vital. You have to establish a straight line across the fabric which needs to be at a right angle to the selvedge. With a loosely woven fabric, you can do this by pulling a thread from across the weave. For a tightly woven fabric, you need to use a large set square and long straight edge to cut the pattern straight and at a right angle to the selvedge (see diagram, below). If you are using a fabric with a pattern repeat, the curtains will look best if the repeat is at the bottom of the curtains rather than the top. Always check your measurements twice before cutting. Mark the top of every drop with tailor's chalk. This is especially important for fabrics with a nap, as they should always run in the same direction.

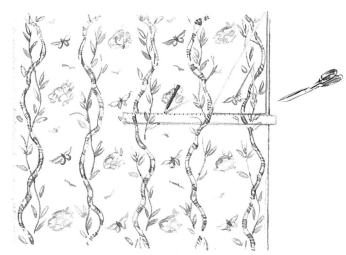

joining widths of fabric

If you have more than one drop in a curtain, widths will have to be joined. If there is a half width, lay the half drop to the outer edges of each curtain. Lay the drops out on the floor, right sides together, and pin 2cm in from the selvedge. Baste, then machine together making an ordinary flat seam. Snip the selvedges at an angle approximately every 10cm to release any tension. Iron out the seam flat (see diagrams, below). When joining widths with a large pattern, first cut the main drop in each curtain, then move the fabric up and down the main drop to work out the match which looks best to the eye before you cut it.

Make sure you cut the second drop for the other curtain to match the first. Pin together the drops, then baste, before machining. Snip the selvedges as previously described.

MAKING UP CURTAINS

weights

Some curtains hang better if they have a little weight added to the bottoms. There are different types of weights available, but broadly speaking you will find lengths of flexible weights (hem tape) in different sizes. Sheers need about 25g per metre, lightweight curtains 70g per metre, and heavier curtains take 150g per metre. These weights should be sewn into the hem of the curtain before it is doubled over and invisibly stitched at regular intervals to stop them slipping (see diagram, below). There are also coin-type weights which are sewn into the corners of curtains (see diagram, bottom).

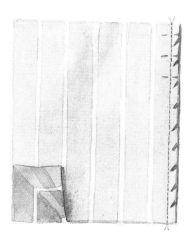

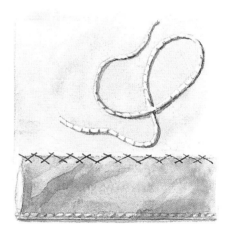

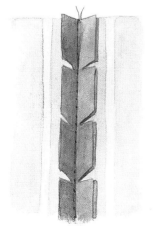

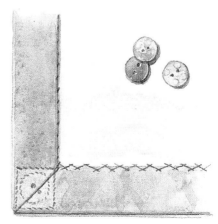

attaching heading tape

Prepare your curtains to the stage where side and bottom hems are finished and the top hem is folded over ready for heading tape. With the curtain on a large flat surface, wrong side up, cut a length of the heading tape about 6cm wider than the curtain. Pin it to the curtain about 5cm from the top (unless a project specifies a greater distance), leaving equal amounts of tape overlapping both sides. For the leading edge of the curtain (the edge at the centre of the window), secure the loose cords of the tape by pulling them out from the back of the tape a little and knotting the ends securely (see diagram, right).

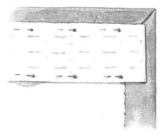

Fold under the end of the heading tape, covering the knotted cords, to just within the edge of the curtain. Pin and baste (see diagram, right).

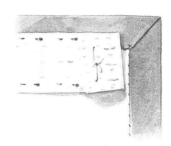

For the outer edge of the curtain, pull some cord through the front of the heading tape and knot off. Fold the excess tape under. Pin and baste (see diagram, below). Machine the heading tape using the following method to keep it completely flat (see diagram, top right).

Sew along the top from A to B, leaving the needle in B, sew down to E. Cut

the thread. Put the needle in at C, 4cm or 5cm from the edge, and machine to corner A, leave the needle in, turn, and sew to the corner D, turn and sew to the corner E, then back up to B. Cut the thread. By sewing the long edges in the same direction, you will prevent any unsightly rucking.

Gather up the tape by pulling the cord evenly to the desired width. Even out the pleats by hand. Wind the excess cord into a neat bundle and stitch this to the tape. NEVER cut this string as you won't be able to flatten out the heading when cleaning or storing. Insert the curtain hooks at regular intervals (about every 10cm). Always have a hook close to the outer edges so that the curtains hang straight. Do not put a hook into the slots with the knitted cord.

hanging curtains

If the curtains are bulky and heavy, it is helpful to have someone else holding the weight of the fabric while you are on the stepladder. Fix the first curtain starting from the middle hook to distribute the weight. Hooks should always be attached to the rings from the front, except the two outermost hooks. These should go on from the back so that the curtain will have a slight inward roll, which is more attractive. Once both curtains are up, close them to make sure they meet and are straight. Then open and ease the gathers into long straight folds. You can tie each curtain loosely with a length of tape in two or three places to hold the folds, and leave overnight.

If the fabric is light coloured or fragile, you could consider attaching a pulling cord to the leading edges of the curtains. These are easily available in a variety of sizes and finishes.

STITCHES

running or gathering stitch

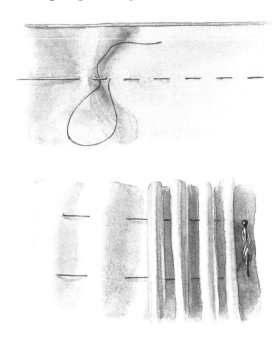

This is a series of neat even stitches, equal in length on both sides of the fabric. Running stitch is used to gather cloth by hand. Knot the thread at one end and sew a straight line along the length to be gathered. Repeat with another row exactly parallel to the first. Wind the loose threads at the end around a pin in a figure of eight and pull gently to form even gathers (see diagrams, above).

basting stitch

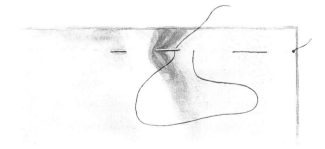

This is a temporary stitch – similar to a running stitch but larger – that holds fabric in place until it is permanently stitched.

Secure the thread with a knot on the wrong side of the fabric, and working from the right side make even stitches about 2cm long through all layers. Use a contrasting colour thread for easier visibility. Try not to machine directly into basting stitches as this can snag the thread (see diagram, bottom left).

slip stitch

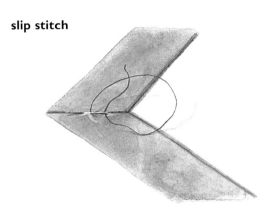

This holds a folded edge to flat fabric or two folded edges together, as in mitred corners. Work on the wrong side of the fabric starting from the right. Start with the needle in the fold. Push it out and pick up a few threads from the flat fabric, keeping the needle parallel with the fold, then insert it into the hem, all in one continuous and smooth movement. The stitches should be almost invisible (see diagram, above).

herringbone stitch

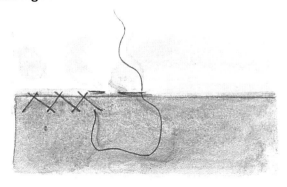

This stitch is used to hold a raw edge to flat fabric. Work starting from the left to right on the wrong side, with the needle pointing from right to left. Start with the needle in the hem. Push it through the hem and bring the needle diagonally up to the flat fabric. Take a small backward stitch to the flat fabric, about 5mm above the hem, picking up just a couple of threads. Bring the needle diagonally back down to the hem, then make a small backward stitch through one thickness of the fabric. Keep the stitches loose (see diagram, previous page right).

hemming stitch

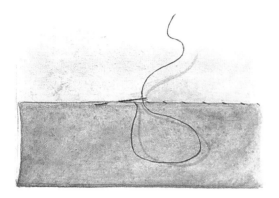

Hemming stitch holds a folded edge to flat fabric. Hand hemming produces a neater finish than hemming by machine. Work on the wrong side of the fabric with the folded edge facing towards you, point the needle diagonally from right to left. Pick up just a couple of threads from the flat piece of fabric. Bring the needle under the folded edge and up through the two layers of fabric. Repeat all along the hem (see diagram, above).

lock stitch

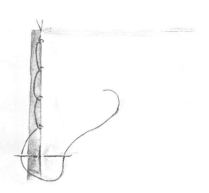

This stitch is used for joining interlining to the main fabric so that all layers are loosely attached. Use long lengths of thread the same colour as the main fabric. Place the fabric wrong side up with the interlining over it. Turn the interlining back on itself and fold along the first width of the fabric. Secure the thread to the interlining and pass the needle through the interlining fold very close to the edge, then pick up a few threads of the main fabric, all in one smooth movement. Keep the stitch loose with a loop and pass the needle through the loop and make the next stitch repeating the loose loop, about 10cm apart. Make sure there is no tension which will pull the main fabric out of shape. This stitch is also used to join lining to the interlining, using the same folding back method (see diagram, above).

cross reference directory

This is an easy cross reference section for techniques and information you will need for making all types of curtains and blinds.

glossary

appliqué a cloth pattern stitched over cloth background

architrave wooden surround of a window or door

batten wooden support for blinds

bay window window projecting from a wall forming an alcove

blackout lining dense heavy lining that blocks light

boss (also called hold back) metal or wooden bracket fixed to a wall to hold back curtains from a window

bradawl sharp pointed tool used for making holes in wood

broderie anglaise usually white or off-white cutwork cotton (or similar)

buckram special material used for stiffening fabric

bump thick soft interlining

casement window vertically hinged window which opens inwards or outwards like a door

chambray fine cotton with white weft

cleat hook used for attaching cord of blinds

domette thin soft interlining

dormer window window that projects from a sloping roof

dowel thin round piece of wood that is inserted into the pockets of blinds to hold their shape

drawn threadwork a technique whereby threads are pulled from the ground fabric to create a geometric pattern.

eyelet metal ring inserted into fabric to form an opening for attaching to a pole or wire

face-fixing where blinds or curtains are fixed outside the recess of a window

finial decorative retaining fixture attached to either end of a curtain pole

gingham checked cotton fabric woven in white with one other colour to create third colour that forms the checks

grosgrain ribbon horizontally corded ribbon

heading tape purpose-made gathering tape to create curtain headings in different designs

interfacing stiffened fabric used for giving shape to curtain headings or seams

interlining a soft material sewn between curtain fabric and its lining, used to give weight, hang better, and for sound and heat insulation. Also known as bump or domette .

leading edge the edge of curtains that meet in the middle when drawn

mitred corner the diagonal join of two piece of fabric, on a corner

organdie finely woven, hardwearing thin cotton which is semi-transparent and lends itself well to pleating

pelmet a decorative top used either for hiding the tops of curtains or to add height to a window, usually made from fabric covered wood.

picot ribbon thick cotton ribbon with decorative edging

piping cord cotton string used as a base for making piping, which is used to outline or edge

portière rod a specially made pole which swings through 180 degrees for use to hang curtains on a door or attic windows

recess-fixing where blinds or curtains are fixed in the alcove of a window

sash-window vertically opening window

scallop ornamental fabric edging of semi-circular curves

selvedge tightly woven edge of fabric preventing it from fraying

template a shape made from paper or card which is used as a pattern to mark fabric

touch-and-close tape (also known as Velcro) double tape, one side of which is nylon hooked, the other side looped, which when put together, form a strong, locking bond. Used for hanging blinds, closing seams, etc.

valance fabric plemet that covers the tops of curtains

webbing tape a strong herringbone tape used between two layers of fabric to reinforce interlining

project credits

P48, graphic roman blind: charcoal wool edging from GP&J Baker; woven linen from Sanderson. P51, bands on tension wire: linen and polka dot fabric from Nya Nordiska; tension wire kit from Habitat. P54, mitred panel: white fabric from Nya Nordiska; border fabric from Jane Churchill. P58, double curtains: checked linen from Colefax & Fowler; printed linen from Celia Birtwell; grosgrain edging from V.V. Rouleaux; double pole kit from The Bradley Collection. P63, appliqué valance: white fabric from Nya Nordiska; blue appliqué fabric from Malabar. P66, swedish blind: fabric from Designers Guild; glass rings with kit from Pax Marie. P71, layered linen panels: scrim from The Natural Fabric Co.; antique blue linen and monogrammed linen from Guinevere Antiques; buttons and embroidery thread from John Lewis; bench cushion fabric from De Le Cuona Designs Ltd; throw cushion on bench from Chelsea Textiles; wallpaper by Neisha Crosland from The Paint Library. P74, patchwork curtains: tea towels from The Linen Cupboard, John Lewis, The General Trading Co. and The Volga Linen Co.; curtain pole and finials from Artisan; metal ring clips from Walcot House; blue metal chairs from Guinevere Antiques. P78, portière panels: fabric from GP&J Baker; portière rods made by J.H. Porter & Son. P82, sliding panels: polka dot sheer from Nya Nordiska; white linen from Malabar; sliding panel system from Silent Gliss. P90, terry shower curtain: terry cloth and sheer lining fabric from John Lewis; trimming from Chelsea Textiles; eyelets and tool from James & Alden; metal hooks from Cope & Timmins. P94, fringed roller blind: ticking fabric from Malabar; cotton fringe from Chelsea Textiles; black velvet ribbon from V.V. Rouleaux. P96, edged wool curtains: wool from GP&J Baker; cream bobble fringe from Jane Churchill; antique wooden pole, rings and brackets from McKinney & Co. P100, unlined curtains with ribbon trim: heavy cream linen from De Le Cuona Designs Ltd, both ribbons from V.V. Rouleaux. P104, contrast lined curtains: black and white fabric from Bennison Fabrics; white fabric from Malabar; poles made by J.H. Porter & Son; wooden table from Decorative Living; radiator covers made by Jali. P108, shaped roller blind: striped fabric from Ian Mankin; trimmings from V.V. Rouleaux. P110, self-valance curtains: fabric from Brunschwig & Fils; trimmings from V.V. Rouleaux. P115, fixed taffeta curtains: silk from Turnell & Gigon. P119, inverted pleat blind: fabric from Bennison Fabrics; velvet edging from V.V. Rouleaux; leather sofa from Highly Sprung. P122, reversible curtain with tie-back: embroidered linen from GP&J Baker; checked cotton from Ian Mankin. P132, sequined blind: fabric from Cath Kidston; sequin trim from V.V. Rouleaux. P136, scalloped curtains: red stripe from Scalamandre; floral cotton from Bennison Fabrics; portière rods from Artisan. P140, quilt curtain: antique quilt from Butterscotch, ricrac trim from Wendy Cushing. P144, simple swag: silk from Malabar; bobble fringe from V.V. Rouleaux. P148, pencil pleat floral curtains: fabric and edging from Cath Kidston; pole from Cope & Timmins. P152, roll-up blinds: striped fabric from The Blue Door; all storage baskets from The Holding Co. P156, ribbon curtain: all ribbons from V.V. Rouleaux; antique beads from Tobias & the Angel; Perspex pole from David Industrial Plastics. P158, pleated organdie curtain: organdie from MacCulloch & Wallis; gingham ribbon from V.V. Rouleaux; pole from John Lewis; wallpaper from Cath Kidston; cot bed from Bump. P162, antique linen curtain: antique linen sheet from Tobias & the Angel; satin ribbon from V.V. Rouleaux; brass pole and brackets from Sasha Waddell. P164, gingham curtains: gingham, chambray and floral trim from John Lewis; velvet violets and grosgrain ribbon from V.V. Rouleaux.

suppliers

Artisan
Tel: 01722 203444 for brochure
Metal curtain poles and finials

Bennison Fabrics
16 Holbein Place
London SW1 8NL
Tel: 020 7730 8076
Printed Fabrics

The Blue Door
74 Church Road
Barnes
London SW13 0DQ
Tel: 020 8748 9785
Fabrics, furniture, accessories

The Bradley Collection
Lion Barn, Maitland Road
Needham Market
Suffolk IP16 8NS
Tel: 01449 722724
www.bradleycollection.co.uk
Comprehensive range of high quality
poles, finials, brackets, tension wire kits,
etc

Brunschwig & Fils
10 The Chambers
Chelsea Harbour Design Centre
Lots Road
London SW10 0XE
Tel: 020 7351 5797
www.brunschwig.com
Fabrics, trimmings, wallpaper, furniture

Bump
Tel: 020 7249 7000
www.bumpstuff.com
Mail order furniture—wooden beds in
kit form

Butterscotch
172 Walton Street
London SW3 2JJ
Tel: 020 7581 8551
Quilts and linen, old and new

Byron & Byron
Vittoria Wharf, 10 Stour Road
London E3 2NT
Tel: 020 8510 4800
Poles, brackets, finials, etc

Cath Kidston
8 Clarendon Cross
London W11 4AP
Tel: 020 7221 4000
www.cathkidston.co.uk
Mail order and branch. Fabrics,
wallpaper, home accessories

Celia Birtwell
71 Westbourne Park Road
London W2 5QH
Tel: 020 7221 0877
Printed fabrics

Chelsea Textiles
7 Walton Street
London SW3 0JD
Tel: 020 7584 0111
www.chelseatextiles.com
Embroidered and crewel work textiles,
trimmings, accessories

Colefax & Fowler
110 Fulham Road
London SW3 6RL
Tel: 020 7244 7427
Fabrics, wallpapers, trimmings

Cope & Timmins
Tel: 020 8803 3333
www.copes.co.uk
Large range of tracks, poles, accesories,
haberdashery & curtainalia

The Curtain Exchange
133 Stephendale Road
London SW6 2PG
Tel: 020 7731 8316
www.thecurtainexchange.net
Branches nationwide. Quality
secondhand curtains

Davis Industrial Plastics
Tel: 01293 552836
Perspex rods

Decorative Living
55 New Kings Road
London SW6 4SE
Tel: 020 7736 5623
Eclectic mix of antiques and made to
order furniture

De Le Cuona Designs Ltd
1 Trinity Place
Windsor
Berkshire SL4 3DE
Tel: 01753 830301
www.delecuona.co.uk
Handloomed linens, silks, paisleys, wools

Designers Guild
275-277 Kings Road
London SW3 5EN
Tel: 020 7351 5775
www.designersguild.com
Contemporary fabrics, trimmings,
wallpaper, furniture & accessories

The General Trading Co.
2 Symons Street
Sloane Square
London SW3 2TJ
Tel: 020 7730 0411
www.general-trading.co.uk
Furniture, linens, household accessories

GP&J Baker
For enquiries Tel: 01494 467467
www.decorativefabrics.co.uk
Fabrics, trimmings, wallpaper

Guinevere Antiques
574 Kings Road
London SW6 2DY
Tel: 020 7736 2917
www.guinevere.co.uk
17th–19th century antiques &
accessories

Highly Sprung
310 Battersea Park Road
London SW11 3BU
Tel: 020 7924 1124
www.highly-sprung.co.uk
Many branches
Sofas, sofa beds & chairs

The Holding Co.
241-245 Kings Road
London SW3 5EL
Tel: 020 7352 1600
www.theholdingcompany.co.uk
Mail order and branches
Everything to do with storage

Ian Mankin
109 Regents Park Road
London NW1 8UR
Tel: 020 7722 0997
Mail order and branch
Fabrics, checks, stripes & plains

Jali
Apsley House
Chartham
Canterbury
Kent CT4 7HT
Tel: 01227 831710
www.jali.co.uk
Mail order. MDF radiator cover kits &
decorative fretwork

James & Alden
Unit 2000
Regis Road
London NW5 3EE
Tel: 020 7278 6860
www.jamesalden.com
Eyelets and tools

Jane Churchill
135 Sloane Street
London SW1X 9BX
Tel: 020 7730 9847
Fabrics, trimmings, wallpaper,
accessories

J.H. Porter & Son
13 Cranleigh Mews, Cabul Road
London SW11 2QL
Tel: 020 7978 5576
Bespoke metalworkers

**John Lewis Department
Stores**
For branches call 020 7629 7711

The Linen Cupboard
21/22 Great Castle Street
London W1G 0HY
Tel: 020 7629 4062
Linens, tea towels

MacCulloch & Wallis
25–26 Dering Street
London W1R 0BH
Tel: 020 7629 0311
Cottons, organdies, silks, velvets,
haberdashery

McKinney & Co.
Studio P
The Old Imperial Laundry
71 Warriner Gardens
London SW11 4XW
Tel: 020 7627 5077
info@mckinney.co.uk
Bespoke curtain poles, etc from glass &
leather to handpainted

Malabar
31–33 The South Bank Business Centre
Ponton Road
London SW8 5BL
Tel: 020 7501 4200
Fabrics: cottons, silks, crewel, and
Kashmir wool

Manuel Canovas
110 Fulham Road
London SW3 6RL
Tel: 020 7244 7427
Fabrics: cottons, silks, velvets and prints
in a large colour range

The Natural Fabric Co.
Wessex Place
127 High Street
Hungerford
Berkshire RG17 0DL
Tel: 01488 684002
Mail order. Fabrics: cottons, linens,
toiles, scrim

Nya Nordiska
2/11 Chelsea Harbour Design Centre
Lots Road
London SW10 0XE
Tel: 020 7351 2783
www.nya-nordiska.com
Fabrics: huge range sheers and extra
wide fabrics, cottons, linens

Pax Marie
35 Walcot Street
Bath BA1 5BN
Tel: 01225 465130
Swedish textiles, furniture, & glass rings
for Swedish blinds

The Paint Library
5 Elyston Street
London SW3 3NT
Tel: 020 7823 7755
www.paintlibrary.co.uk
Paint, & wallpaper

Pierre Frey
253 Fulham Road
London SW3 6HY
Tel: 020 7376 5599
Fabrics: prints, cottons, velvets, weaves,
trimmings

Sahco Hesslein
24 Chelsea Harbour Design
Centre
Lots Road
London SW10 0XE
Tel: 020 7352 6168
www.sahco-hesslein.com
Fabrics-very modern textiles

Sanderson
233 Kings Road
London SW3 5EJ
Tel: 020 7351 7728
www.sanderson-uk.com
Fabrics, wallpapers, accessories

Sasha Waddell
3 Sandilands Road
London SW6
Tel: 020 7736 0766
www.sashawaddell.com
Brass curtain poles, furniture and
accessories

Scalamandré
Unit G4
Chelsea Harbour Design Centre
Lots Road
London SW10 0XE
Tel: 020 7795 0988
www.scalamandre.com

Shaker
72 Marylebone High Street
London W1 3AR
Tel: 020 7935 9461
www.shaker.co.uk
Mail order. Furniture & accessories in
Shaker style, homespun linen

Silent Gliss
01843 863571
www.silentgliss.com
Large range of modern curtain tracks
and panel systems

Tobias & the Angel
68 White Hart Lane
Barnes
London SW13 0PZ
Tel: 020 8878 8902
Mail order. Antique furniture, textiles,
accessories & furniture made to order

Turnell & Gigon
Unit M20

Chelsea Harbour Design Centre
Lots Road
London SW10 0XE
Tel: 020 7351 5142
Fabrics: cottons, velvets, linens, prints,
trimmings

**Valerie Brooks Bespoke
Curtains**
14b Wilcox Road
London SW4 6SP
Tel: 020 7720 0011
Bespoke curtain makers

The Volga Linen Co.
Unit 1D
Eastlands Road Industrial Estate
Leiston
Suffolk IP16 4LL
Tel: 01728 635020
www.volgalinen.co.uk
Linen by the metre, sheets, tea towels
& accessories

V.V. Rouleaux
54 Sloane Square
London SW1W 8AX
Tel: 020 7730 3125
www.vvrouleaux.com
Trimmings, ribbon, haberdashery

Walcot House
Lyneham Heath Studios
Lyneham, Chipping Norton
Oxon OX7 6QQ
Tel: 01993 832940
www.walcothouse.com
Modern metal poles, rings, tabs, ready
made curtains & eyeletting service

Wendy Cushing
Unit G7
Chelsea Harbour Design Centre
Lots Road
London SW10 0XE
Tel: 020 7351 5796
Huge range of trimmings and tassels

index

Figures in bold refer to projects; figures in italics refer to captions

author acknowledgments

I have been most fortunate in being able to photograph in the homes of friends who have let me invade with curtains and blinds and people. They include Suzanne and Chris Sharp, Martine and Nick Criticos, Gabi and Pierre Tubbs, the Harrington family, Marylin Phipps and Martin Butler, Seskin Kelly: thank you, one and all!

Many thanks to David Hiscock for terrific photographs that belie the most ghastly weather in which some of them were shot. A real pro. Lizzie Sanders has produced exquisite water colours of the projects – each one a work of art. Thank you Lizzie!

Of course, making up all these projects required large amounts of fabric, most of which was generously given to me, and thanks go to: Trudi Ballard at Colefax & Fowler, Antonia Lake at Malabar, Cath Kidston, Jilly Newberry and Louise Laycock at Bennison Fabrics, Angela Childs at Celia Birtwell, Elizabeth Henderson at Butterscotch, Matthew Gomez at Turnell & Gigon, Sue Avery at Scalamandré and Emma Wilcock at GP&J Baker. The curtains needed tracks and poles and I am indebted to the following people for their generous help: Ali Edney at The Bradley Collection, Matthew Robinson at Silent Gliss, all at McKinney & Co., Sasha Waddell and Nanuschka Jackson – thank you all.

Valerie and Jim Brooks made many of the curtains and blinds for the book. Thank you both for your extraordinary kindness, humour, and professional input. Helena Lynch also made many of the projects with her usual efficiency and intelligence. Alexandra Martins and Catherine Coombes provided enormous help and support during the shoots – many thanks.

At Quadrille, many thanks go to Françoise Dietrich for her sensitive art direction and help, and to Nicki Marshall and Alison Moss for taking control of the text! Thank you to Lucinda Ganderton for her technical help with the projects. And of course to lovely Jane O'Shea for making this happen.

In memory of Ronald Abrahams who was such a help in flooded Normandy.

photo acknowledgments

1–5 David Hiscock; 6–7 Verne Fotografie/architect Jo Crepain; 8 View/Sally-Ann Norman; 9 Marie Andersson/©Stiftelsen Skansen; 10 The Interior Archive/Fernando Bengoechea; 11 The Interior Archive/Andrew Wood/designer Alison Henry; 11 inset far left Verne Fotografie; 11 inset far right The Interior Archive/Fernando Bengoechea/designer Glenn Gissler; 11 inset left Richard Glover/architect Ian Hay; 11 inset right Camera Press/*Sköner Hem*/IMS; 13 Deidi von Schaewen/designer Gaetano Pesce; 14 Minh & Wass Photography/designer Betsey Johnson; 15 *Marie Claire Maison*/Nicolas Tosi/Josée Postic/Renault/designer Jacqueline Morabito; 16–17 Minh & Wass Photography/architect Pierce & Allen; 18 Christian Sarramon; 19 *Marie Claire Maison*/José van Riele/Karin Scheve; 20 Alexander van Berge/Menno Kroon; 21 Minh & Wass Photography; 22 centre Andreas von Einsiedel; 22 left Marie Andersson/© Stiftelsen Skansen; 22 right Andreas von Einsiedel; 23 The Interior Archive/Edina van der Wyck/designer Charlotte Scott; 24 left IPC/© *Homes & Gardens*/David Montgomery; 24 centre Ray Main/Mainstream; 24 right Alexander van Berge/designer Wim van de Oude Wetering/*Elle Wonen*; 25 left Christian Sarramon; 25 right David Hiscock; 26 left Richard Glover/architect John Pawson; 26 right Narratives/Jan Baldwin/architects Melloco & Moore; 26–27 The Interior Archive/Edina van der Wyck; 28–29 Christian Sarramon; 29 centre Christian Sarramon; 29 left Deidi von Schaewen/architect Gilles Bouchez; 29 right The Interior Archive/Frtiz von der Schulenburg/designer Jean-Louis Germain; 30 Ray Main/Mainstream; 31 centre Verne Fotografie/architects Robbrecht & Daem; 31 left *Marie Claire Maison*/Christoph Dugied/Josée Postic; 31 right Didier Delmas/designer Roberto Bergero; 34–41 David Hiscock; 42–43 Marina Faust/courtesy AD France/Les Publications Condé Nast; 44 above left Christian Sarramon; 44 above right *Marie Claire Maison*/Marie-Pierre Morel/Josée Postic; 44 below left Minh & Wass Photography/designer Betsey Johnson; 44 below right Mark Seelen/designer Winka Dubbeldam; 45 above *VT Wonen*/photographer Grootes; 45 below *World of Interiors*/Alex Ramsay/designer Diane de Clercq; 46–85 David Hiscock; 86–87 The Interior Archive/Simon McBride; 88 above left Didier Delmas/designer Bénédicte Laglenne; 88 above right Red Cover/Andreas von Einsiedel; 88 below left Minh & Wass Photography; 88 below right *Marie Claire Maison*/Christophe Dugied/Josée Postic; 89 above The Interior Archive/Fritz von der Schulenburg; 89 below Lars Hallén; 90–128 David Hiscock; 128–129 *World of Interiors*/Simon Upton; 130 above left Narratives/Polly Wreford; 130 above right Marie Andersson /©Stiftelsen Skansen; 130 below left IPC/© *Homes & Gardens*/James Merrell; 130 below right *Marie Claire Maison*/Nicolas Tosi/Julie Borgeaud; 131 above The Interior Archive/Andrew Wood/designer The Cross; 131 below The Interior Archive/Henry Wilson/artist Celia Lyttleton; 132–175 David Hiscock.